# "A NORTH-EAST COAST TOWN"
## ORDEAL AND TRIUMPH

THE STORY OF KINGSTON-UPON-HULL
IN THE 1939-1945 GREAT WAR

BY

## T. GERAGHTY

*(By courtesy of the Hull and Grimsby Newspapers Ltd.)*

HOWEN:
HULL ACADEMIC PRESS
2002

Published by
Hull Academic Press
5–7 Vicar Lane
Howden,
East Yorkshire
DN14 7BP

ISBN 0 946289 45 X

1st Edition 1951 by Kingston upon Hull Corporation
2nd Edition by Kingston upon Hull City Council
Reprinted 1989 by Mr Pye (Books)
Reprinted 2002 by Hull Academic Press

© 1951 Kingston upon Hull City Council Reprinted by permission.

Printed and bound by Bell & Bain Ltd., Glasgow

# PREFACE

## by COUNCILLOR SIR LEO SCHULTZ, O.B.E.
### Leader of the Kingston upon Hull City Council

The Civic and Parliamentary Sub-Committee of the City Council have asked me to write this Preface. *A North-East Coast Town* was published in 1951, but the paper shortage meant that it was only possible to print 2,000 of the 30,000 copies originally planned. The book has been out of print for some time and this reprint has been prepared in response to the many requests from all over the world.

I am sure that the present generation will appreciate the history of this period in the life of our City. The ordeal of the citizens during the time of almost continuous aerial bombardment and the fortitude of the inhabitants in the face of enemy attacks makes a glorious page in the saga of our City. It was a proud boast of the people that, in spite of the heaviest raids and the serious devastation of household and commercial property, "no ship from this port ever missed a tide".

Tribute should be paid to the work of the late T. Geraghty, the Assistant Editor of the Hull Daily Mail, who collected the material and wrote this stirring account of the work of the civil defenders as a mark of the gratitude of the whole of the City.

Perhaps I can best illustrate the spirit of the ordinary people, their courage, their fortitude and, above all, their irrepressible good humour which enabled them to defy the worst that an implacable enemy could inflict upon them, by telling a true story of the period. After a night raid upon a working class district I accompanied the Regional Controller, Gen. Sir William Bartholomew, on a visit to the damage. At one house which was completely destroyed, a woman, black with the soot that soiled everything after a raid, was searching among the rubble for the small household goods, the letters and the photographs which were all that remained of yesterday's home. The General asked her where her husband was and, quick as lightning, received the illuminating reply—"In Libya—the coward!"

Shortly after the heaviest bombing the Corporation demonstrated its faith in the future of the City by engaging two of the country's greatest planners, Sir Edwin Lutyens and Professor Abercrombie, to draw up a scheme for the post-war reconstruction of the City. In doing so it matched the courage of the people with its steadfast and unshakable confidence that the City would rise like a phoenix from the ashes when the devastation of war was replaced by the reconstruction of peace.

May the memories of those dark days, brightened by courage and hope, be revived by a re-reading of this epic account. May the record inspire a new generation to fresh endeavours, to realise a finer city worthy of a gallant people.

Leo Schultz.

March, 1978.

# INTRODUCTION

## HULL'S MARTYRDOM

The purpose of this book is to tell posterity of the self-sacrifice, heroism and steadfastness of the civilian population of Kingston upon Hull who volunteered to serve in one capacity or other for the rescue, welfare and immediate future of the aged, sick and lame, the women and children of this great Port and City when it became a focal point for attacks in the World War which began in September, 1939.

How they enrolled, trained and served under the most bitter conditions, facing death on innumerable occasions and in intense blackness will be recorded in separate chapters, but an idea of the circumstances under which they worked as volunteers can be gained from the fact that during the war there were 82 raids during which high explosive and incendiary bombs were dropped.

> People killed numbered about 1,200.
> Injured 3,000.
> Houses damaged 86,715 (leaving only 5,945 undamaged).
> People rendered temporarily homeless and provided for 152,000.
> Number of alerts, 815.
> Hours under alerts, over 1,000.
> 250 domestic shelters and 120 communal shelters were destroyed, from which more than 800 people were rescued alive.

The book is published under the authority of the Hull Corporation not in any spirit of aggrandisement, but as a tribute to those who served whether as a professional man or woman, a labourer or a housewife, and an incentive to future generations to serve their fellows under like conditions of terror.

T. G.

General Sir William Bartholomew, G.C.B., C.M.G., D.S.O.
Regional Commissioner, 1941-1945.

# FOREWORD

By Sir William Bartholomew, G.C.B., C.M.G., D.S.O.,
Regional Commissioner for the North Eastern Region, 1941 to 1945

The Chairman of the Emergency Committee for Kingston upon Hull—Mr. Russell—has honoured me by asking me to write a short Foreword to the History of Civil Defence in the City.

Victory in Europe has come and Hull with its great docks, which were so heavily attacked, stands to-day terribly scarred, but with the knowledge that great services have been performed throughout the war for the Nation.

I accept the Chairman's request with the greatest pleasure, for I have been filled with admiration for the tenacity, the patience and the bravery of the citizens of Hull.

Never once, even during the long period when German bombs fell almost daily and still more frequently at night, did the citizens waver in their determination to see it through and to keep the City, its port and its factories in full activity. There was never any reduction in essential work, except in areas where damage after raiding had to be repaired before work could go on.

Many citizens, men, women and children, forfeited their lives or were terribly injured, but their fellow citizens stood firm. The wonderful women were undaunted and kept their homes going often in conditions which had to be seen to be believed.

It must not be forgotten that in 1941 many of the worst bomb attacks were concentrated on the crowded portions of the City and on the dock area. The City suffered perhaps as heavily as any other in the country in proportion to its size during the intensive period of German attack on the Humber.

I have seen the City with great fires raging in many places and devastation widespread, but the idea of its people throughout was defiance, often expressed in best Yorkshire amid scenes of ruin and fire. This courage, this determination, bravery and cheerfulness was a wonderful thing to meet and a great help and encouragement to the leaders who were engaged in the work of setting the City on its feet again.

Then I should like to pay a tribute to the fine Civic leaders—the Lord Mayors of the City whom I have known during the war for their calm and efficient leadership which did much to match and supplement the great qualities of the people—one of them, Alderman Schultz, throughout the years of war an active member of the Emergency Committee and Deputy Controller.

It has been my privilege to work closely with all the members of the Emergency Committee. They thought, and thought rightly, that it was their duty, not only to plan and organise the defence of the City against the German attack, but also to supervise the operations of the Civil Defence Services in action and to lead during actual attack. Under their able Chairmen, Councillor Speight and Councillor Russell—the former was also Controller during the height of the German attack—the Committee worked as an efficient and united team. An outstanding example of their work was the post-raid reorganisation after the heavy raids in March and May, 1941. Aided greatly by the assistance of the soldiers brought into the town, the City was quickly ready to meet the next attacks which followed at once. I am also convinced that the Emergency Committee's insistence on the policy of dispersal of shelters, and small ones at that, was instrumental in saving many lives.

As for the work of the officials and members of the Civil Defence Services headed by the Controller, Mr. Speight, of the Police, the Fire Service, the W.V.S. and Allied Services, no praise is too high for all alike, from the messenger boys and girls to the highest ranks for their efficiency, bravery and initiative. Many members of these services, sad to say, lost their lives or were seriously injured; I am sure they will always take a high place in Hull's roll of honour. I can only add that I am proud to have been associated with them all and record my admiration for the achievements of both full-time and part-time members.

In conclusion, I wish the City of Hull great prosperity, and that the problem of restoration may be successfully solved with results which will be worthy of its great-hearted people.

*W. H. Bartholomew.*

## TO THOSE WHO SERVED

In World War II commencing September, 1939, there were 82 raids in which high explosive or incendiary bombs were dropped within the boundaries of Kingston upon Hull.

| | |
|---|---:|
| People killed numbered, so far as known | 1,200 |
| Injured, and received treatment | 3,000 |
| Total damage incidents | 146,568 |
| People rendered homeless, and dealt with | 152,000 |
| Houses destroyed or damaged | 86,715 |
| Number of alerts | 815 |
| Hours under alerts, more than | 1,000 |

Official announcements over the B.B.C. and in the Press scarcely ever referred to Hull by name. It was always a "north-east town." Hence, as a tribute to the steadfast courage of the people, who kept the City and Port going through following their normal occupation by day, and turned out by the thousand in the impenetrable darkness of night to volunteer as Civil Defence workers in duties for which they had spent countless hours in training, this book is published.

It is Hull's pride that in spite of almost incredible strain and suffering imposed on the community, the Luftwaffe never held up the working of Hull either as a port or a city for a single day.

This, then, is the City's tribute to the men and women, boys and girls, of all classes, who stood the test and won through it. Their example should be an inspiration to future generations.

## MEN WHO ACCEPTED RESPONSIBILITY
### LORD MAYORS AND SHERIFFS DURING THE WAR

| | *Lord Mayors* | | *Sheriffs* |
|---|---|---|---|
| 1939 | William Pashby. | 1939 | Wallace Rockett. |
| 1940 | Henry Melville Harrison. | 1940 | Benno Pearlman. |
| 1941 | Sydney Herbert Smith, M.A. | 1941 | Robert Greenwood Tarran. |
| 1942 | John Guy Hewett. | 1942 | Godfrey Robinson. |
| 1943 | Joseph Leopold Schultz. | 1943 | George Stanley Atkinson. |
| 1944 | Frederick Roland Fryer. | 1944 | Harold Ivens Loten. |
| 1945 | John Dewick Lambert Nicholson. | 1945 | Kenneth Percival. |

## CIVIL DEFENCE "NERVE CENTRE"
### WHAT WENT ON AT "CONTROL"

The Headquarters of the Civil Defence Services of Kingston upon Hull acted as a sort of godmother and godfather to all the various services, and, indeed, individuals in the City. It was from here that appeals for volunteers were launched, training schemes started, 210,000 civilian respirators despatched, contacts made with Regional Headquarters, all reports of "incidents" received and passed to the particular service

## MEMBERS OF THE EMERGENCY COMMITTEE

Coun. W. O. Honor.  Ald. Frederick Holmes.  Ald. A. Stark, O.B.E.  Coun. F. Chapman.  Coun. Gordon Russell, O.B.E.
Coun. Leonard Speight, O.B.E. (Controller).  Ald. J. L. Schultz, O.B.E. (Deputy Controller).  (Chairman).

needed. In addition, it became the first place sought for an answer to countless thousands of inquiries. The inquirers may have had to be despatched elsewhere, but it was to "Control" that in the main they came first. In one period of a few days in the May raids of 1941 more than 10,000 telephone calls on the operational side alone were dealt with.

Let us look, then, at the mass of material available, and extract some salient facts from the Controller's report.

The Air Raid Precautions Committee, as it was then known, had a number of meetings before 1937, and in 1938 was really at work, though its activities were receiving scant attention from many. The crisis in September of 1938 made all citizens really alive to the danger, and though there were numerous offers of help, Munich came and went by. It set fears at rest, but the A.R.P. Committee went on with its plans for the provision of shelters, static water tanks and reception centres, the building up of the Warden Service, the formation of Rescue and Decontamination squads, the measures necessary for evacuation. Parades were held, publicity was embarked upon, blackout exercises were held, training classes of every description formed, and Government instructions put into operation. It was disheartening work, for the war had not yet arrived, yet it went on. Since then the people of Hull have had cause to be grateful that it did, though actually it was not until March, 1939, that the Committee which was to bear such heavy responsibilities came into being under the decentralisation scheme of the Government, which had appointed Regional Commissioners. The first for the North-Eastern Area was Lord Harlech, who was succeeded by Sir William Bartholomew.

## THE FIRST SIREN.

The Controller's report shows that Hull's first warning in this war came at 2-45 a.m. on Monday, September 4th. It was an "Air Raid, Yellow," and all operational staffs went to their posts. The public siren did not sound until 3-20 a.m., the "Raiders Passed" going at 4-8 a.m. Many thought that it was a needless alarm, caused by some nervous person. The falsity of this belief is proved by the time expiring between the receipt of the message and its conveyance to the public. As a matter of fact, there was a further "Alert" conveyed to Control that morning, though it proved to be a stand-by only, and not for public information. November 21st brought the last alert of 1939. The next was not to come until June of 1940. Even so, the members of the A.R.P. Committee were meeting every day except Sundays to keep equipment up-to-date, and maintain the various services at the highest efficiency.

Though there had been "incidents" in the near neighbourhood at farms and the like, the first recorded incident in the boundaries of the City came at 11-13 p.m. on June 19th, 1940, when, after explosions caused by gunfire, an incendiary bomb brought a fire in a field at Marfleet. A little more than an hour later incendiaries were showered on East Hull, Victor Street, Buckingham Street, and the immediate neighbourhood being the target. There were a few high explosive bombs, but little damage was done, at any rate compared with what was to come.

## FIRST DAYLIGHT ATTACK.

A fortnight later, July 1st, East Hull was to have the first daylight raid in the country, a lone aircraft crossing the City at 5-30, apparently undetected until too

Alexander Pickard, C.B.E.,
Town Clerk.

C. H. Pollard, O.B.E.,
City Treasurer.

Wm. Morris, O.B.E.,
City Engineer.

Dr. N. Gebbie,
Medical Officer of Health.

late to give a warning. The roar of the guns was the first intimation people had of impending danger. That plane set fire to the oil tanks at Saltend, details of which are given in the chapter dealing with the Fire Fighting Services.

Although information had been received of the German intention to use parachute mines, the first one did not arrive until 1-40 a.m. on October 22nd, when a mine dropped at the end of Strathmore Avenue, Beverley High Road, near the River Hull. Two mines were actually dropped before the warning was sounded, bringing extensive damage to hundreds of houses and many casualties, two of which proved fatal. The power of the explosion can be gleaned from the following facts known to the writer : A man getting dressed was lifted to the ceiling of the bedroom, and then found himself on his bed in the front room downstairs. The blast had stripped him of his pyjamas.

By this time the City had heard considerably more than a hundred alerts, those in the daytime causing a hold-up in works, offices and factories. Hence a system was evolved by which the " alarm within the alert " could be given by means of a telephone department installation. The pressing of a button showed that danger was imminent, whereupon workers went to shelter. Records show that in more than a thousand hours of public alarms 268 hours only were under the " alarm within the alert." Thus the working hours at which men were able to remain on production, knowing that they would be warned when danger was imminent, were beyond count.

Up to the end of 1940 Hull had not suffered badly, though the unending warnings were putting people on edge through sleepless nights, and anxiety over danger to come. There was, too, the upsetting of business routine, for one day the sirens sounded six times, and on another occasion there were eight individual preliminary warnings. However, 1941 was to bring heavy losses and almost overwhelming responsibilities. On February 4th there was an attack on Goddard Avenue, with heavy casualties in proportion to the damage done. The following day there were six public alerts without an attack, and six more attacks before February was out. One of these brought the first serious trouble with an unexploded bomb, which fell near a railway, closed an important engineering works, compelled scores of people to leave their homes for temporary accommodation, and generally interfered seriously with the life of the Newington area. These raids brought also machine-gun fire, a new experience, and more land mines, one of which failed to explode in Ellerby Grove.

March 1st brought a parachute mine attack on East Hull, James Reckitt Avenue, the most bombed thoroughfare in the City, figuring in it. In every attack the people at Control expected the name of James Reckitt Avenue to crop up. It generally did. March 13th was the date of a sustained attack which necessitated the calling in of outside help for the first time. Stoneferry was the target that night, while on the following night a land mine fell in Bean Street with very heavy losses and damage.

## HEAVIEST RAID TO DATE.

At 8-11 on the evening of March 18th the sirens sounded. Half an hour later chandelier flares were suspended in the skies, making the City a perfect target, and at 9-45 the first bomb fell on an oil-extracting factory. Later on a gas undertaking received considerable damage and had to cease service ; the electricity generating station received another unexploded bomb, and there was an urgent call for it to be dealt with on priority. More than a hundred high explosive bombs were dropped, 700 houses were rendered totally uninhabitable, and another 700 vacated temporarily.

Robert G. Tarran,
Chief Warden.

T. Wells,
Chief Constable.

Miss Doreen B. Mason,
Senior Woman Warden.

Mrs. Morton Stewart, M.B.E.,
Joint Organiser,
Hull Women's Voluntary Services.

Thirty unexploded bombs were reported, roads were blocked or torn up, 700 fires were started (though many were dealt with without the aid of the Fire Services), and, most important, heavy casualties caused. The death roll that night was over 90.

## CONTROL H.Q. DESTROYED.

Monday, March 31st, was the night on which Control H.Q. was totally destroyed with loss of life and the destruction of valuable records. The site was at the corner of Ferensway and Spring Bank. The public warning went at 8-20 and flares dropped shortly afterwards. This was a sign of a heavy raid, which actually began a few minutes after nine, East Hull fire station suffering. Flares, high explosives and land mines fell in almost every section of the City, water mains being broken, roads blocked by falling buildings, the main streets strewn with glass, and 200 casualties registered, 50 of them fatal. Five hundred houses were made uninhabitable, while another 2,000 were damaged. Several industrial undertakings were also put out of action.

It was towards the end of the raid, somewhere after 10-15, that a land mine fell outside the Shell Mex Buildings, Ferensway, which housed Control H.Q. Inside was the Deputy Medical Officer of Health, Dr. Diamond, who was handing over his duties in connection with the Casualty Services to Dr. Wheatley, the newly-appointed Civil Defence Medical Officer. Dr. Diamond was killed, as was a policeman on duty outside. All that was found of the policeman were pieces of his uniform. Fire-watchers on an upper floor were other fatalities.

The blast swept the staff in all directions, wounding some, rendering others incapable of action through shock. Ceilings fell, walls caved in, fire broke out. Furniture, filing cabinets, typewriters, etc., were piled in indescribable confusion, rendering the vacation of the falling and blazing structure most difficult. Yet there were some who stayed on to try and fight the small fires or to give the layout of the building to the rescue parties. Official cars parked outside were blown sky high, a concrete section of the roadway stood up vertically, and valuable, almost irreplaceable, documents were lost.

Yet, somehow, Control was functioning before dusk fell the next day.

## PUBLIC SHELTER STRUCK.

April brought a number of raids of a minor calibre to those previously experienced, but on the 15th a parachute mine fell on a crowded public shelter in Ellis Terrace, Holderness Road. Nearly 200 casualties were registered, of which number 60 were killed or missing. Then, following other warnings, raids and attempted raids, came the tragedy of May, 1941.

## THE MAY, 1941, RAIDS.

On May 7th, 1941, after an almost seven hours warning on the previous night, the sirens went at 11-16, and at 12-35 the first H.E. bomb fell in Cleveland Street. It is believed that when the real serious news of the raid was realised every man and woman in the Civil Defence Service, whether on rota duty, on reserve, or free from duty, reported to his or her headquarters, despite bombs, shrapnel, or the almost impossible task of traversing roads except on foot. This made it possible, within two hours, to halve parties, thus dealing with two incidents instead of one. The elder among the school children, boys and girls, even turned out to act as messengers, and

D. BELLAMY, O.B.E.,
Manager, Electricity Department.

T. H. JONES,
Water Engineer and Manager.

ANDREW RANKINE, O.B.E.,
City Architect.

G. H. PULFREY,
Transport Manager.

since normal means of communication were either destroyed or partly out of action, their services were most welcome.

For the purpose of this record it may be as well to deal with the two raids of May 7th-8th and May 8th-9th as one happening, but for those who like to have official times, the stand-by on the first night lasted from 11-16 to 5-8 ; on the second from 12-5 to 5-55.

It is known that upwards of 300 high explosive bombs were dropped, these including parachute mines and " G " bombs. Some 40 of them failed to explode, though each one was a menace for a considerable time. The incendiaries, from flares to oil bombs, numbered thousands. There were 2,600 wardens on duty each evening, many of them becoming casualties, six, unfortunately, fatal. In addition, many of their posts were damaged, some utterly destroyed, which meant the immediate setting up of a new centre, since the wardens, men and women, could not work without a base.

Four-fifths of the telephone system was put out of action, and in the eastern sector only five official phones were available. Nearly 130 Rescue parties operated, some of them consisting of military parties, which meant that the City Engineer, who was in charge, had 1,500 personnel to direct. They attended more than 100 incidents, on which 70 rescue operations were required, and reached nearly 700 persons. Two hundred and seventy-nine were dead.

The Casualty Service had had upwards of 600 staff on duty and nearly 100 vehicles for first-aid party work. They took 550 casualties to first-aid posts or the hospitals, where magnificent work was done while the raids were on, sometimes in buildings bereft of roofs and windows and even on fire. Doctors attended people who were wounded and trapped by falling girders, women ambulance drivers drove through walls of fire to reach their destinations or convey their patients somewhere for treatment. There was no place of safety. With the sounding of the " All Clear " came mobile canteens distributing hot drinks and food to working parties and the homeless. They had made their preparations during the raid, not gone to shelter.

EIGHT HUNDRED FIRES.

During the two nights hundreds of fires were put out by members of the various services and the general public as soon as the incendiary bombs began their fell work. Even so, the fire brigades had to deal with approximately 800 conflagrations. The City Centre, King Edward Street, Jameson Street, Prospect Street, became a mass of flames, most of the large stores, hotels, restaurants, and numerous small shops being destroyed. Industrial plants in all parts of the City suffered damage, as did the Guildhall, the City Hall, and Prudential Buildings at the corner of King Edward Street. The high tower of the Prudential Buildings had to be demolished the next day for public safety.

Wholesale and retail markets were destroyed, as were warehouses and office property. The Riverside Quay was gutted from end to end, timber stacks blazed sky high, sending sparks in vast circles to ignite other property. Rank's flour mill was put wholly out of action, 3,000 dwelling houses were either wrecked or seriously damaged, 9,000 had doors and windows torn out of their frames, and 50,000 suffered minor damage from blast, bomb or shrapnel. The telephone department had 14,000 faults to deal with, though their administrative office was destroyed ; a main cable containing 2,000 pairs of wires was put out of action, while a direct hit from a high

J. H. Ward,
Cleansing Superintendent.

J. Cranshaw,
Information Officer.

T. Holme,
Telephone Manager.

J. H. Pilling,
Fire Force Commander.

explosive set fire to the main Corporation bus depot, destroying a number of double-deck vehicles. All that was left were the blackened walls and a tangled mass of iron. The coal gas supply in East Hull ceased, 200 mains having been damaged and others flooded by water. The Electricity Department had 6,000 calls to deal with " faults," but the general supply of electricity was maintained except in areas immediately surrounding the point of impact. Railway lines were hit at many points, and several suburban services were out of action for some time, making an extra call on the buses available.

Bread supplies in some districts were affected, but assistance from out of town soon eased this source of worry.

## MERCY WORK OF W.V.S.

In those two nights more than 40,000 people had to be helped, the homeless shepherded to reception centres, terrified children pacified, scattered relatives put in touch with each other. The work was done efficiently and so humanely that the reputation of the Women's Voluntary Service for the part they played in this connection soared to great heights. After those nights the members of the W.V.S. had a real place in the hearts of the people. Round that time, too, 9,000 people were evacuated under the control of the Director of Education and his department. The casualties on those two nights totalled 1,200, 400 being fatal. In 36 cases identity could not be established.

So many were unidentified or unidentifiable that on May 12th there was a communal funeral for 200. To avoid crowds the impending ceremony was not made known to the general public, but the tragedy and grief of the relatives present was so poignant and overwhelming that it was decided never to repeat the ceremony if any possible means existed to avoid it.

The main roads were open to traffic two or three days later, a considerable achievement when it is remembered that there were blockages or craters at 160 places, while on 50 roads passage was quite impossible.

Before closing this chapter, it is but fair to say that Hull became greatly indebted to the 2,000 military who helped by taking on rescue work, directing traffic, demolishing dangerous buildings, and running transport, and to the many East and West Riding fire units who responded to the calls for assistance. It is also worth mentioning that officials of the Dogs Home and the R.S.P.C.A., with other animal lovers, dealt with 700 domestic pets, not hesitating to enter dangerous buildings to rescue them or deal with them otherwise.

Before midnight on the 9th the sirens went again, and a third night of terror was expected and prepared for. Happily, few of the enemy made landfall, and with the exception of a few bombs at Sutton little happened except the strain of a five hour stand-by for officials and civilians alike, all of them at a point of exhaustion.

On the 13th Clifton Street, Albany Street, Beverley Road and Princes Dock were hit, and on the 29th South-West Hull in the region of St. Andrew's Dock and Dairycoates, fortunately with few casualties. Thus ended a May never to be forgotten during living memory in Hull.

## DEATHS AFTER " ALL-CLEAR."

June 2nd brought the fiftieth raid, and though it was only small, it had most unfortunate results. The " Raiders Passed " signal had sounded, and people were

R. C. Moore,
Director of Education.

D. J. T. Bagnall,
City Analyst.

H. G. Freeman,
Director of Social Welfare.

making their way from shelters to their home when bombs dropped in Park Grove, Cave Street, Blenheim Street, Marlborough Avenue and Margaret Street. The list of dead totalled 27, all killed within a matter of minutes when they thought they were safe. The 23rd of the month brought a small attack, and the 29th a heavy one in East Hull. It was during this raid that the Deputy Chief Constable (Mr. James Smith), on duty in a car driving to a bombed site, was struck by a splinter which went through the body of the car and killed him.

June and early July brought a number of small attacks, but the tempo stepped up on July 11th when the central and south-western areas were attacked. This raid brought nearly 150 casualties, 21 being fatal. On the 15th a raid of similar proportions, this time in North-West Hull, meant death for 25 people and injuries to more than 50.

The last really heavy raid occurred on July 18th, 1941. In the course of a few hours, or as a result of wounds received during them, nearly 150 people died. Direct hits were registered on Rank's flour mill, East Hull gas undertaking, and Messrs. Reckitt's factory. It was during this raid that there took place the disastrous incident at Franklin Street shelter, Holderness Road. The General Post Office was hit, as were more than 200 industrial buildings, Crowle Street police station, and the Y.P.I., George Street. Approximately 7,000 houses received damage of a more serious description than broken windows, 1,500 being made uninhabitable.

On the night of August 18th, 53 people were dealt with by the Casualty Services, 20 being dead, and on the 31st, 44 were killed and 59 attended at hospitals or first-aid posts. More than 1,000 houses were damaged in that visit.

## HULL'S BIGGEST BOMB.

The first three months of 1942 were fairly free from raids, and opportunity was taken of the quiet to clean up and patch up, as well as revise the various services, training the new-comers who replaced those called up for National Service. The season began on April 13th with a raid on West Hull, and then came May again. On the 19th probably the biggest bomb ever dropped on Hull descended on Scarborough Street, a densely-populated area near the Fish Dock. Nearly 200 people became casualties; 50 of them were killed. The material damage was beyond assessment, for a vast area was flattened, while blast damaged countless houses and shops beyond temporary repair.

As the months followed there were a lessening number of raids, though there was always strain and anxiety after the sounding of the sirens. On December 20th, unfortunately, the warning did not sound until after bombs had dropped, people being killed in the Marfleet Avenue. It was the last raid of 1942.

## THE BUTTERFLY BOMBS.

January, 1943, was but three days old when the sirens went, again after bombs had been dropped, and the 15th brought another visit which made the Gas Identification Service busy with phosphorous bombs, but this was followed by five blessed and almost unbelievable months of freedom. June 24th brought the first attack of anti-personnel, or Butterfly Bombs, insignificant looking weapons with great destructive power if handled or disturbed. They were so small that they could get into any crevice. Happily their coming had been prepared for and the public well informed of their character. Hence, although there were nigh on 100 casualties, including

The City Centre—Pre-War.

Once a Hull landmark, this gaunt tower of the Prudential Assurance Building was all that survived after fire and explosions had wiped out King Edward Street (City Centre).

A later view of the City Centre.

22 dead, there was not a serious incident created through inquisitive people handling anti-personnel missiles. The casualties came from high explosive and the like.

The night was, however, extremely serious from the fire standpoint. Central Hull was the target, the streets to suffer being Bond Street, Jarratt Street, Albion Street, Savile Street, etc. It was the night that the Royal Institution, long the centre of much of Hull's cultural life, was destroyed. The main fire station was also involved. A thousand houses were damaged, 400 seriously.

July 14th, 1943, brought the last heavy attack on the City by enemy planes. It was heavy in character, 24 being killed and 72 injured. The enemy dropped a considerable number of high explosives and phosphorous bombs, with a liberal supply of incendiaries, many of the latter of the explosive type. One serious happening was the destruction of a road over a rail bridge, which caused considerable dislocation of road and rail traffic for some time.

As a sort of final gift, Hull was on the route for a number of flying bombs destined for West Yorkshire and Lancashire. One of these dropped on the outskirts of the City, but happily in a field, the only damage being to windows and roofs from the blast. Since the date was December 24th, the visit was a most untimely one from the point of view of the householders who had to patch and mend their property in time for Christmas.

Actually it took more than six months to repair damage caused by this bomb, which was very extensive. Some of the houses were badly shattered.

## THE WARDEN SERVICE

" The Gay and the Gallant " is an expression used many times in history to describe a body of men famed for their skill at arms, their gallantry in action, or their abandon in social matters. To no body of men and women is the phrase more appropriate than to the men and women of Hull who manned the Warden Service in the great trial befalling the people from 1939 to 1945. Gay, gallant, aye, generous and gentle also. To no one who lived in the City in that phase of history will their memory be ever anything but one to be held in honour, respect and affection. They were the men who knew most things, or, if they did not, at any rate knew how to get to know the answers to the puzzles regarding rations, forms, leaves, pensions, railway trains and the like, in the hours and days of waiting for the horror which was to come. They saw to the bandaging, tunnelling, transport to hospital, the making of hot beverages, the checking of residents in a neighbourhood so that no one should be left buried alone, even the provision of a temporary home when calamity did come.

On paper the services of the Wardens consisted of reporting incidents and giving assistance pending the arrival of other Services. In reality they did a thousand things, not only at the moment, but for days afterwards. Before long this meant that the Warden was accepted by the public, not only as a neighbour, but as a personal friend. This began shortly after the beginning of the war, and became solidified on that night in June, 1940, when the first H.E. bombs fell. It has lasted ever since and will continue, though the armlets, uniforms and steel helmets are put away. It will continue to last.

Some reasons why ?

Well, on the night of April 16th, 1941, a parachute mine dropped on Ellis

Premises in Jameson Street reduced to a heap of rubble.

Terrace, Holderness Road, a very thickly populated area. A public shelter received a direct hit, all the occupants being killed and 500 rendered homeless. Notwithstanding the ensuing devastation, which made the district like a battlefield, the Wardens rescued the dead with the reverence due to them, consoled the relatives and guided them to places where they could be attended to and comforted until permanent arrangements could be made for the interment of the dead and practical assistance rendered.

A few weeks later, on the night of May 7th-8th, 1941, a five storey factory building was involved in a raid. More than 500 people were in shelter there. Two parachute mines were dropped in the vicinity, one on the east side, one on the west. Though there were no fatalities in the factory itself, most of the occupants had lost their homes. Yet, despite the fact that the whole City was undergoing one of the most severe raids of the war, hot tea was provided and temporary accommodation found.

On the very next night a parachute mine dropped in the backways of 37th Avenue, North Hull, causing casualties, trapping victims and wrecking homes, yet within the hour the Wardens had done their work so efficiently that it was possible to withdraw the personnel.

On July 18th, 1941, high explosive bombs fell in Mulgrave Street, an industrial area, thickly populated. Factories were hit, shelters pulverised, 30 people killed, 130 injured, and more than 800 rendered homeless. Again the Warden Service, members of which had their own personal and domestic worries, rendered inestimable service in the hour of stress and undertook heavy responsibility in post raid work, checking the missing, the wounded and injured, helping in compiling forms and claims, without which aid illiterate and uneducated people would have been bewildered.

In the same month, nay, the very same night, an incident occurred at the corner of Franklin Street, Holderness Road. A shelter received a direct hit, a Wardens' post was moved several feet by the force of the explosion, a cinema and a bank destroyed, to mention a few of the results and ignoring the thousand less graphic but very important personal experiences, involving loss of furniture, valued intimate possessions, domestic pets and the like, through all of which, until order was produced out of chaos, the Wardens carried on, setting aside all personal calls and even mental anxieties.

Such close contact with the people, allied with their facility for calming and quieting the alarmed, their ability to deal with incendiary bombs, fight small fires and give immediate attention to family and domestic affairs, made the Wardens far more than Government or civic officials enrolled for the duration of the war for an emergency. It made them neighbours, even close family friends, who could be trusted and whose decision could be relied upon with confidence. What the Wardens could not do personally, merely inspired them to find someone who could.

Add to all this very practical help, despite the dangers in times of real stress and strain, their work in maintaining morale, their concerts, Christmas parties and entertainments, sometimes involving the booking of a whole theatre for a visit to a pantomime, charitable work of an extensive character for those who would accept it, and one realises why the Wardens of Hull are, and ever will be, held in respect, admiration and often affection, especially as their assistance did not arise in any haphazard way, but was the result of skilled organisation, through the Chief Warden,

Prospect Street. A main Shopping Centre. Many Casualties occurred in this area. The Royal Infirmary (in background) was severely damaged.

Another view of Prospect Street.

Post Leaders, and on downwards to the man and woman who was content to be a mere fetcher and carrier, skilled in no special way, but merely ready to render help and voluntarily submit to discipline for the good of the whole.

## THE SAFETY FIRST MAN

After one raid a warden in the Fountain Road area saw a man carrying rubbish across the road, and asked him his business. The man replied that he was filling up a hole in the road before someone fell in it. Actually it was the resting place of an unexploded bomb !

## WARDENS STRENGTH

The highest approved strength of the Warden Service was 3,459 part-time men and women and 801 full-time. The highest actual figures were 3,282 and 733 respectively. The total number of persons passing through the Service was over 6,500.

## FED 400 ON 14/2

Extract from an East Hull Warden's report during the May, 1941, blitz :

" One reception centre had a direct hit—it was Hedon Road Wesleyan—so I opened out Churchill Street Junior School. There were 2,000 homeless, but we had a Queen's Messenger canteen there. I went back to my District and carried out after-raid routine. At 11-15 I found that no food had arrived at Churchill Street, so I sent a messenger to Divisional Headquarters to see if there was anything doing.

Reply came through, ' You are the boss. Do something.' So I bought food. I asked the people round about for anything they had to spare and had a lot given. I bought the food from the Seamen's Institute, which had been damaged. I only spent 14/2. The people were splendid, especially since theirs is a very poor district."

Then the writer found that 13 of his wardens were homeless. He was one of them. So they lived gipsy fashion, scrounged pots and pans, made a fire, and were then all right !

# RESCUE

Like so many brave men, the members of the Hull Civil Defence Rescue Service are very modest about their activities and accomplishments, even though these involved the most exhausting labours, sometimes while bombs were falling, always with the possibility of a house or a wall crashing and burying the men with those they were trying to rescue. To obtain even a pin-point view of their work we have to depend on stories from other sections of the Civil Defence Services and of the rescued themselves. For an example of the latter, read the following letter from a schoolgirl, only try to visualise the picture as the girl saw it :

THE RESCUE ADVISORY COMMITTEE.
Consisting of representatives of the Corporation, the Master Builders' Federation and the Building Trade Operatives.

" Dear Rescue Men,

Just a few lines thanking you for what you did for us on July 14th, 1943, how you helped to get my mother out, and to get my to brothers which was dead, how you help me to get to the shelter when I hedent any shoese to my feet. I went to fetch you when stuff was falling, well men you did very well to work through it like you did when gunfire was on, well men keep a good hart like me.

To the Rescue men from Joyce

with love and kisses for all."

Not a letter to win a scholarship, but certainly one to move any heart to compassion.

## THE HULL LIFT METHOD.

The personnel of the Rescue Service were essentially building trade operatives well versed in constructional work, knowing all about struts and stresses. A few began training as early as January, 1939, and in the course of time they mastered every phase of their particular job and were able to give courses to British and American Army units as well as to Civil Defence and Fire Service men. Their efficiency was such that their headquarters were raised to the standard of a Regional School, and a method which they invented of lifting collapsed shelter roof slabs was accepted by the Ministry of Home Security and circularised throughout the country as " The Hull Lift Method."

Several hundred " incidents " were attended, the usual practice being to send two teams of ten men each. The average time taken to complete the rescues was ten hours, but there were occasions when six parties (sixty men) worked continuously for three and four weeks to make certain that the body of every person killed had been recovered.

It was not, of course, work that could be rushed. A hasty act, or a badly handled pick or shovel, could easily bring down an already shaky wall, making the condition of the buried worse than it was before. Tunnels had to be dug and the sides buttressed, men had to crawl and claw through soil and clay, with perhaps a leaking gas pipe close at hand, and on winter days and nights lie in water which chilled their very bones. It needed cold, calculated courage as well as technical skill, apart altogether from the fact that much of the work was done while a raid was in progress, or during a period when the " Alert " was in operation, thus forbidding the use of any worth-while light. Even hand torches had to be used with the greatest care.

## TERRORS FACED.

Altogether, thirteen members of the service were awarded decorations or commended for their services. Had ten times that number been recognised it would not have been too many for the people of Hull, for there were times when these men, most of whom followed their ordinary building trade avocation during the day, had to have their clothing dampened to prevent them catching fire.

Fire, gas, mud, water, falling buildings, tunnels, complete darkness, all have their terrors as single units. The men of the Hull building trades, organised as Rescue workers, faced them as a combination, and more often than not successfully accomplished what they had set out to do—save people from suffocation and death under piles of rubble.

All that was left of Messrs. Thornton-Varley's shop premises, Brook Street Corner.

No more dancing on this roof dance hall of Hammond's Ltd., which fed one of the most spectacular fires of the war.

## A BOMB CENSUS

It is not generally known, though it should be, that during the war the Hull City Engineer and his staff accepted, as an extra to their normal work and war work, a charge from the Home Office to give a census of the bombs which fell.

To give a number would have been a simple task, but the information required and given covered the following details : the time of the fall of the bomb ; the estimated size ; whether exploded or not ; the size of the crater and the type of soil ; the location and notes on the damage. These notes included information on the type of buildings totally destroyed or so seriously damaged that demolition would be necessary ; those seriously damaged but capable of repair later ; the number of casualties from each bomb, and whether they were fatal, seriously injured or slightly injured, and finally whether the victim was a man, woman or child. Lastly, a sketch, designed so that it could be fitted on to an ordnance map of the City, was supplied so that Home Office officials had first-hand information at their disposal in the clearest possible manner.

In addition, information was supplied to the Research and Experiments Departments concerning 47 " special incidents," all involving considerable detailed work.

## AN EXPERIMENT IN DEMOLITION

The duty of deciding whether a damaged building should come down, or could be shored up, fell to the technical assistants of the City Engineer and the experts of the military under the Chief Naval Engineer. It was an onerous and responsible task, for the public had to be safeguarded yet buildings saved if possible.

In this latter respect there was an interesting and successful experiment in the case of the mill in Wincolmlee of Messrs. Chambers & Fargus. The walls only were damaged, the roof being quite sound. Hence it was decided to jack up the roof and support it temporarily on large tanks within the building. The damaged walls were pulled down by wire ropes attached to steam rollers and were rebuilt, and the roof was jacked into position on them. In a comparatively short time the mill was again brought into use.

On the other hand, the Prudential Tower, a landmark in the heart of the City, had to be demolished by explosives. It fell precisely on the pre-determined line !

Hundreds of shops and business premises, damaged or severely shaken by nearby bomb blast, were inspected and instructions given regarding their safety for use.

## SALVAGE

To most people salvage means the recovery of paper, rags, cinders, tins, old pans, and the like. To the City Engineer's Department of the Hull Corporation it meant the handling of bricks, steel, wood from premises damaged or destroyed by bombs, or blackened and twisted into seemingly impossible shape by fire. The garnering was done from within shaky walls always likely to fall because of insecure foundations

Another large store is gutted—Messrs. Edwin Davis' premises, Bond Street.

The Guildhall received a direct hit.

or the whims of the wind. The material was needed for runways for aerodromes, roadways for barracks, machine gun strong points for the military, and other essential works for both defence and offence, as well as civilian needs such as sites for hutments for the homeless.

One way and another, half a million tons of brick rubble and debris were handled, the good bricks being recovered, as well as 7,500 tons of iron and steel, 610 tons of lead and other non-ferrous metals, 3,000 tons of timber, and 5,000 tons of firewood, all to find a place somewhere in Britain's war effort.

In all, the demolition of some 1,000 hereditaments were completed, besides many large commercial buildings in busy and often narrow thoroughfares.

Another task undertaken under this head was the collection, removal, and storage of household goods from raid damaged property until the owners found a new abode, a business not always accomplished in a matter of hours or days. Sometimes the goods were redelivered to places miles away. The value of such service to displaced people can only be imagined.

During the May raids so large was the demand for accommodation that despite the requisitioning of as many halls and schools as were available, open-air dumps had to be used with specially released tarpaulin sheets for protection. There was an inventory of all goods handled, and a special guard to prevent unauthorised people enriching themselves.

Following the raids of May 7th-8th and 8th-9th, 1941, the articles in 2,809 homes were dealt with. Yet thanks to the system prepared and followed no difficulty was experienced in tracing the movements of the furniture or other household contents.

Among other types of goods salvaged from damaged warehouses were valuable food stocks such as syrup, sugar, cocoa beans, grain, and tinned goods of all descriptions and cash to the value of nearly £2,000 was involved. In one instance £800 in £1 notes were recovered from debris, and in due course handed to the surviving relatives of the owner after Letters of Administration had been taken up.

Happily the discharge of often dangerous but always most valuable work was carried out without either a fatality or even accident of a serious nature.

# SUCCOUR FOR THE WOUNDED

## WORK OF THE CASUALTY SERVICES

During the course of the war 3,907 men, women and children were tended by the staff of the Medical Officer of Health for Hull. Of these just under a third were dead. The others were either admitted to hospital or treated at first aid posts. These cases were, of course, additional to the ordinary accidents likely to happen in a large community. What plans were made to meet the emergency, and how were they carried out?

In between the wars the local branch of the Red Cross Society had been in abeyance, had almost, indeed, ceased to function, but it was expected that the officers and men of the St. John Ambulance Brigade would provide the nucleus of the Casualty Service. True, they were keen enough to do so, but when the calamity came it was found that owing to the call-up of man-power, the long stretches of duty which men had to put in at their employment and in other causes, there were not available the

Dr. Diamond, Deputy Medical Officer of Health, and a policeman on duty were killed when a heavy bomb seriously damaged this Building in Ferensway, which housed the A.R.P. Control.

numbers expected. Hence a start had to be made, if not from zero, from pretty well close to it. For example, although 46 buildings were set aside as first aid depots or posts, it was possible to man only 21 of them.

## 2,817 VOLUNTEERS.

So a recruiting campaign was launched, and the courses of instruction which followed produced a gradually increasing roll of trained personnel which, at about the height of the raids, totalled 2,546 certificated men and women out of 2,817 who had volunteered.

These met the first rush of casualties, and the effect on public morale of their display of calmness and authority, the staunching of blood, the cleansing of a grime-besmirched face, the bandaging of a wound, etc., cannot be over-estimated. People in distress quickly realised that they were not to be left to their own devices, that succour on the part of trained people was at hand and would be given lavishly. Remember that all who came suffering from shock of some sort were in the main dust-covered and dirty; that others bore gaping wounds or crushed limbs, were perhaps unconscious; that some had to be given morphia; that all had to be labelled and docketed, and made to feel that they were persons of some importance. Moreover, all this work, whether of a routine character or demanding initiative and immediate decision for good or ill, had to be carried out while bombs were still dropping and guns booming perhaps a matter of a hundred yards away. On one night alone, at one depot seven members of the staff were killed and four wounded.

About these men and women who worked under almost incredible difficulties, sometimes at a point of physical exhaustion, the Medical Officer comments in his report: " I have never had cause to complain of the work of the First Aid Parties, or of the staff at the First Aid Posts. Casualties among them have, I fear, been more common than honours and awards, but the men and women in the Service have the satisfaction of knowing that they have done a grand job, and that they have deserved and received the gratitude of those whom it has been their privilege to help."

## THE AMBULANCE STAFF.

More than 130 vehicles were engaged on full-time service for the conveyance of the wounded to hospital or of the dead to the mortuary. The drivers and attendants, many of them mere girls who had perhaps been at work all day, met the first shock since they had to deal with distracted parents or relatives, calm the patient, perhaps carry him on a stretcher over heaps of rubble, and drive back through black streets with even the possibility of a crater ahead, and with fragments of shells falling around and sometimes on their vehicle.

Apart from sitting cases, these men and girls conveyed 1,115 seriously injured to hospital. How many there are now living who might have bled to death without this service is beyond conjecture. More than that number (1,205) were conveyed to the various mortuaries, to be cleaned and prepared for burial by members of the staff of the Medical Officer.

Altogether, 11 members of the Casualty Services were killed, one being Dr. D. Diamond, the Deputy Medical Officer of Health, who was on duty at the Control Centre at the time. Twenty were injured on duty. Seven first aid centres were struck during raids, and more than a dozen ambulance vehicles destroyed or put out of action.

## HOSPITALS STRUCK

As all five main hospitals in Hull were within a vulnerable area, being either near the railway station or the docks, the Medical Officer, with an official of the Ministry of Health and the Medical Officer for the East Riding, made arrangements for casualties to be sent to two hospitals on the edge of the City for first treatment, and for two base hospitals, at Beverley and Driffield respectively, to receive the more serious cases in a matter of hours. The aim was to save patients from being exposed to further bombing.

The wisdom of this dispersal, never at any time an easy business, was proved on several occasions, for each of the five hospitals in the City was damaged more or less seriously. Anlaby Road Hospital was hit three times, on one occasion 330 beds being put out of use. At Beverley Road Hospital, on March 18th, 1941, an H.E. bomb meant that 74 beds had to be vacated. Hedon Road Hospital was struck four times, having in the May of 1941 to be vacated except for a matter of 30 beds for emergency purposes. The first aid post, however, continued to operate! The Children's Hospital in Park Street had a number of bombs near-by, to suck out or blow in windows and damage the roof. The Royal Infirmary, on March 31st, 1941, had a visitor in the shape of a parachute mine near the end of a wing, which damaged three wards and made useless 157 beds. Two months later incendiaries and blast from high explosive placed the Infirmary out of commission as a receiving centre, though later two small wards were repaired and reopened for urgent cases and air raid casualties. The Out-Patients' Department first aid post and the Orthopaedic Department remained in use. Then at both the Sutton Annexe of the Infirmary, and at the City Hospital at Cottingham, bombs fell within the grounds, though happily without doing any structural damage.

## A DEEP DEBT.

Two surgical teams and one resuscitation team were allocated to each receiving hospital once a raid was on, and of them the Medical Officer of Health writes somewhat too modestly, but in accordance with medical tradition : " The service rendered by the doctors was all that could be desired." Could man write less or mean more ? The people of Hull know how deeply indebted they are to those who carried out the almost herculean task of building from almost nothing a magnificent organisation of paid and unpaid men and women, doctors, nurses, first aid workers, ambulance drivers, cooks, ward maids, mortuary attendants, and others who rendered a great service, not only efficiently, but with humanity and graciousness.

# SALUTE TO THE POLICE
## THEIR JOB AND THE COST

It is the duty of a policeman to come to the assistance of honest folk in time of need. It is for that that he is trained and, in time, given authority. Normally, however, he has stated hours. In wartime and particularly during the raid periods, these pretty well went by the board so far as the Hull Constabulary and their comrades of the Special Constabulary were concerned.

The regulars accepted the stopping of their periodic leave (one day off in seven), worked twelve hours a day during danger times, studied anti-gas measures and how

# THEIR MAJESTIES THE KING AND QUEEN VISIT THE CITY, 1941

THE ROYAL PARTY WITH THE LORD MAYOR AND SHERIFF IN A BOMB-DAMAGED AREA OF THE CITY.

HANDSHAKE BY HIS MAJESTY FOR WOMEN WARDENS AND MEMBERS OF THE W.V.S.

# THEIR MAJESTIES THE KING AND QUEEN VISIT THE CITY, 1941

The King and Queen chatting with Mr. T. W. T. Hammerton (Manager, East Hull Gas Company and a Head Warden).

The King meets the Divisional Wardens.

to deal with unexploded bombs pending the arrival of experts, perfected themselves in first aid work, confounded the ways of despicable looters, and the activities of after-dark law-breakers, and absorbed thousands of Government Orders regarding emergency legislation and Defence Regulations.

They had also to find billets for thousands of soldiers who came to the City, assist in evacuating more than 6,000 people whose lives were in peril from unexploded bombs, undergo training as searchers for anti-personnel bombs, direct traffic and guide civilians at a time when many life-long residents did not know their own City or did not know how to get to a point at which they were aiming.

COOL AND CALM.

During all the stress and strain the policemen of Hull maintained their usual spirit of cheerfulness and helpfulness, somehow learning to " suffer fools gladly " to an astonishing degree. Their coolness and calmness when surrounded by frightened women and children immediately after a bomb had dropped, perhaps while gunfire was still in progress, as well as their courtesy on point or patrol duty during the whole night, went a great deal of the way towards maintaining and even building up the morale of the people.

At times they had to call for help from both the East and West Ridings, and once had the assistance of a hundred soldiers to direct traffic, but on the whole the Hull Police Force discharged the job that came to them on their own—and did it magnificently.

It cost them the lives of seven members of the Force, including that of the Deputy Chief Constable, and the temporary loss of the services of 37 colleagues wounded during air raids. It brought one British Empire Medal, two King's Police and Fire Brigade Medals, five commendations from His Majesty the King, and two letters of appreciation from the Regional Commissioner as well as thirteen commendations from the Chief Constable.

FIRST ON HAND.

There are numerous records showing that a policeman was the first on the spot following the dropping of a bomb. His business then was to bring control out of chaos, work with the wardens, give instructions as to which particular branch of the Civil Defence Services had to be sent for, whether it be Ambulance, Fire, Rescue, or Demolition.

Sometimes he was first in the house or building struck, sometimes he took a hand in keeping under control a fire likely to grow to great proportions or get a ladder to rescue people from upper stories, and sometimes he gave first aid.

Once a constable burrowed on his stomach for four hours, making a tunnel through which the rescue of a woman was effected. On another occasion a sergeant, seeking missing people, found eight children sheltering in a gas cupboard in their night attire. Their ages ran from three months to 15 years. He retrieved their clothing, dressed them, and handed them over to others for safe keeping while he went on to another job. A young constable, having extinguished some incendiary bombs, was resuming his normal patrol when a stick of high explosives fell near. He was knocked unconscious, had both his jaws broken, was blinded for weeks, had three fingers and a wrist fractured, and when in hospital had a hundred stitches inserted in his face and body. Yet he was on duty again in six months !

PERSONAL COURAGE.

A regular constable, with the assistance of a special constable, rescued five people from some vaults, though the roof was continually sagging and debris had to be scraped away. It took them four hours, working in a confined space, the only light available being a pocket torch. At all times there was the likelihood of the roof falling and burying them, but they made the rescue!

The leadership and initiative of another officer led to the saving of hundreds of tons of food and merchandise when three trains were ablaze on a dock quay, though bombs were falling the whole of the time. They took the links off blazing wagons, used their shoulders for shunting, dragged down heavy tarpaulin sheets from wagons to place over burning wheat. Where the wagons were of the closed van type the constable climbed aboard and broke the locks of the sliding doors so that the combustible material could be got at.

Throughout the war the Special Constables worked faithfully and often gallantly alongside their regular colleagues. They, too, did patrol work and traffic direction duties, having their own administrative officers. One section did especially valuable work as a mobile section, providing their own cars for the purpose. Nor must mention be omitted of the 30 auxiliary police women who performed duties as drivers, clerks and shorthand typists, often while raids were on, or of the youths of 16 to 20 who formed the auxiliary messenger service as volunteers. All carried out their allotted tasks, and a deal more besides, steadfastly and with a tenacity of purpose which won the highest regard, not only of those who came into close contact with them, but of the general body of citizens.

## TERRORS THE FIRE SERVICE FACED

When the European situation began to look really gloomy the strength of the Hull Fire Service stood at 72 officers and men. It was then there began a look round to see how the 23 square miles of the City, the 275 miles of streets, the 600 acres of storage ground round the docks, the 12 miles of quays, and the river front of 7 miles, could be protected in the event of concentrated raids.

An early decision was made to allocate sites for sub-stations and institute a patrol system, under which a unit would cover a specified number of streets during an alert and report to its parent station on the completion of the circuit of the beat. Then came the augmentation of heavy fire-fighting supplies, the training of recruits, provision of trailer pumps and vehicles to tow them, an increase in water supplies and means of communication, the appointment of administrative staffs, and a thousand and one technical details of which the general public is necessarily unaware.

The first plan was not rigidly adhered to. It was made elastic so that it could fit into developments or be scrapped if needed, but it was the plan which in course of time enabled the Fire Fighting Service to master 464 fires in one night and 375 the very next. These took place on the nights of May 7th-8th and May 8th-9th, 1941. It shows that the plan was set on a sound basis.

What should be added, however, and that immediately, is that the plan could not have been successful without the courage, loyalty, and endurance of all who donned a fireman's uniform in those dread years. Without those qualities Kingston upon Hull would be a land of waste, good neither for buildings nor agriculture, for altogether 4,910 fires of a major or minor character raged in Hull between September 3rd, 1939, and the cessation of hostilities.

Happily for Hull the enemy gave us time, for the first war-caused fire did not come until March 5th, 1940. Actually there were three, as the result of incendiary bombs, but they were soon extinguished. From then began the almost unending stand-by on the part of the regular firemen, and the constant reporting on the part of the auxiliary men. In four days of that same March, raids caused 25 fires. On the night of June 19th there were fifty.

### PETROL TANK PIERCED.

The first blaze to attract the real attention of the population and to test the Fire Services came in the afternoon of July 1st, 1940. A lone raider running over the City from west to east made a few sporadic attacks at barrage balloons, and then dropped a stick of bombs directed at the Saltend oil installation. He scampered out to sea, not knowing that he had made a lucky hit, though happily for Hull not a crippling one.

The majority of the bombs fell outside the oil installation, but pieces of shrapnel from one bomb pierced the sides of a tank holding about 2,500 tons of petrol, which spurted out of the holes and caught fire. The flames licked the outside of the tank, bringing the temperature of the petrol inside to a dangerous degree, and burning petrol began to flow to a number of adjacent tanks.

Such a situation was enough to frighten the stoutest heart, for there were dense clouds of black smoke ascending to obscure the tank from the fighters. An explosion would have blown to eternity every man in the neighbourhood, and have had tremendous repercussions through the City. Occasionally it looked as though long tongues of flame would bring this about, but despite the heat, the fumes, the blinding smoke, the task was faced and mastered.

### FOUR GEORGE MEDALS AWARDED.

This was achieved through perfect co-operation on the part of the Works fire brigade and the City brigade, allied to the technical knowledge of the experts. Water was projected on to the adjoining tanks to cool them until the arrival of sufficient stocks of foam, when a concerted effort was made to extinguish the fire. Before this was accomplished quantities of petrol had been drawn off and led away, a process which added to the numerous hazards the firemen were accepting as part of their job.

Lack of space here prevents the telling of the full tale of this heroic struggle to save Hull. It is recorded in the official account of the Fire Services story. How grave the position was can, however, be gleaned from the statement that the fighters saved more than 2,000 tons (not gallons) of petrol in the affected tank, apart from the vast quantities in peril in adjacent holders. That was the night on which the first George Medals came to the City, two to members of the staff, two to firemen.

Yet terrible as were the risks run in mastering this fire, it might have happened in peace time. The men were not hampered by the dive-bombing of enemy machines, they were not thrown to the ground by blast or hindered and wounded by hurtling bomb splinters. They did not see their comrades hurtled from great heights while plying the hoses, to be killed or maimed. Nor were their pumps and appliances turned into a heap of useless iron and rubber, as was to be the case later, either at a fire or on the way there. These things happened many times.

THE PRIME MINISTER, WITH THE LORD MAYOR AND SHERIFF, VIEWS AIR RAID DAMAGE IN THE CITY, NOVEMBER, 1941.

PEOPLE DINED AND DANCED HERE BEFORE POWOLNY'S RESTAURANT IN KING EDWARD STREET WAS SWALLOWED UP BY THE FIRE BLITZ OF 7TH/8TH MAY, 1941.

A crew despatched to a fire with a pump attached to a motor car or taxi-cab had to get there. If they saw a blaze on the way they sped on, reporting the new fire when they reached their destination. Thus H.Q. knew where help was, and where help was needed. The winter night assignments were, of course, through dark streets sometimes shrouded in fog, over thoroughfares which might contain craters made since the men were despatched. One man had the uncanny experience of being lifted on a fire escape to find himself seemingly alone in the world. On the ground was a dense mist. Where he was the view was quite clear. He could see everything above the mist, nothing below it.

## FIRST EXPLOSIVE INCENDIARIES

In the early morning of December 12th, 1940, when the first explosive incendiaries were dropped, a building in Alfred Gelder Street caught fire. It was one of forty in the City. The threat was so grave that several units were despatched to counter it. As the water flowed from the hoses sheets of ice formed across the street, firemen could not keep their feet, lengths of hose became frozen, the men lost their balance trying to hold them—yet they fought through to triumph and saved the nearby Guildhall. That same day men rowed in small boats to put out fires on barges in the middle of Prince's Dock. When all was quiet it was found that the hoses were so frozen that they could not be rolled up, but had to be carried in long lengths and thawed out at the various stations !

Another terrifying experience that month was on December 24th, at a High Street warehouse of Messrs. Saner and Harrison. The building had a storage capacity for 20,000 tons of grain and castor beans. At the time it had a known storage of 6,500 tons of wheat besides castor beans. The surroundings, the most ancient part of Hull, consisted of narrow streets and staithes. The water in the Old Harbour was low and could not be used to any great extent. Floor after floor collapsed under the weight of shifting grain, lines of hose were buried under burning embers, the narrow streets prevented the firemen getting away from the heat and the danger of falling walls, but they stuck to their task until the firefloat, the *Clara Stark*, could be brought into action from the water side to pump over 2,000 gallons of water a minute for many hours. More than 120 officers and men were employed on the fire which, when mastered, had to be watched for days to keep down the glow in case of enemy action.

## BEACON FOR BOMBERS.

Four o'clock in the morning of February 2nd, 1941, brought another mill fire in Cleveland Street. The building impregnated with oil from crushed seed over a number of years, consisted of five storeys adjoining a silo of five storeys. The resultant blaze can be imagined, but by tenacious work the fire was cut off, though the mill and silo could not be saved.

After that there was something of a lull from enemy attacks, but March 1st brought the biggest raid to that date. Incendiaries and flares were dropped, then came high explosive bombs.

The control room was inundated with calls, one to a warehouse at North Bridge containing 20,000 wooden crates. It was difficult to get at and an effort was made to gain access through a small window at the top by means of an extension ladder. As it was brought into use the building was dive-bombed. One bomb fell alongside

BURNT OUT BY INCENDIARIES IN MAY, 1941, WERE THESE IMPOSING PREMISES OF W. H. SMITH & SON.

NOTHING OVER SIXPENCE ! ! !   IN FACT, NOTHING AT ALL, AFTER HEAVY EXPLOSIVES STRUCK WOOLWORTH'S EAST HULL STORE.

the ladder and three firemen were killed. At another fire three oil tanks were damaged, the thick oil flowing over the street making it impossible for men to walk.

In Sculcoates a paint works was ablaze, a varnish tank having been ignited by incendiaries. This occurred at the height of the raid, and the tanks acted as a beacon to the enemy planes, one of which dropped a land mine with some accuracy. That night there were 101 fires, 60 of them of major proportions.

So the story goes on of schools, shops, churches, mills and house fires being tackled with the greatest fortitude, despite the lack of rest. One night a unit had its crew buried under the debris of a building which collapsed while the men were on the way to another blaze. A squad of the Rescue Service on the way to an incident released them. The firemen found that their pump had been destroyed and the towing vehicle damaged. They walked back to the station and immediately went out again with a light pump. On the way they were stopped a number of times by piles of debris which the driver failed to see owing to the dense mist, and once by broken telephone wires becoming entangled in the wheels of their car ! It often happened that a crew had to turn round and go another way because of blockages in the streets.

That particular night there were 85 fires, and assistance had to be called from outside areas.

March 31st, 1941, brought 31 fires, among them the building at the corner of Ferensway which housed the Headquarters of the A.R.P. Control Centre. It was the target for a land mine which created vast destruction. The same night another land mine destroyed the Metropole Hall in West Street, while in the Boulevard district St. Wilfrid's Church, school and presbytery were wiped clean out.

April brought a number of raids, that on the 13th causing 67 fires, which brings us to the never-to-be-forgotten month of May, 1941.

## SUCCESSIVE NIGHTS OF TERROR

A raid of small dimensions took place on May 3rd, 1941, a number of land mines being dropped, one severely damaging the Marfleet works of Messrs. J. H. Fenner, belting manufacturers, and another leaving its mark on Alexandra Dock. There were several outbreaks of fire, but none approached serious dimensions. Every night, however, round about dusk there was an air raid warning, with a resultant stand-by till about dawn. There was always the chance that an enemy plane would drop bombs when passing over Hull on the way out to sea !

May 7th appeared to be similar to previous nights, and the warning sounded shortly after eleven. Each station went through the normal routine, but for a period there was nothing more than a few searchlights to attract attention, and not much of that, for it was a brilliant moonlight night.

Suddenly the air was rent with the opening roar of the guns of the anti-aircraft batteries, and shortly after midnight flares began to drop. Incendiaries and high explosives quickly followed. Obviously it was to be a raid of serious proportions.

The first fires were reported from Montrose Street, followed by reports from Chapman Street, Cleveland Street, Spring Bank, Wright Street. Very soon the telephonists were overwhelmed with messages from all parts of the City, and the Regional Fire Officer at Leeds was informed of the position.

The water mains had gone, this in the early stages, so use had to be made of the reserve supplies.

BOMB'S EYE VIEW OF RECKITT & COLMAN, LTD. AFTER A HEAVY RAID ON EAST HULL IN JULY, 1941.

RECKITT'S FACTORY IN DANSOM LANE, SEVERELY DAMAGED IN AN EAST HULL ATTACK.

## SCIENTIFIC FIRE-RAISING

At 1-10 reinforcements were asked for. The District Scheme was put into operation, the first brigade to arrive being the near-by Haltemprice service.

Enemy planes were dropping all known types of bombs, at first incendiaries predominating. As the night went on it became evident that the technique of the raiders was to start a small fire with an incendiary or oil bomb, and then to use high explosives to damage surrounding property and blow the fire through broken windows. An open roof would act as a chimney, helping to create an upward draught. Often the result was that before a fire unit arrived the building was a blazing inferno.

What was more, the enemy had selected a time when the river water was low. As already reported, he had struck the water mains with some early projectiles.

Soon there were a hundred fires, some in the centre of the City being of mammoth proportions. On all the roads leading to the suburbs houses, schools, churches, garages, warehouses and other buildings were ablaze, and further reinforcements were asked for. In a number of cases fire-fighting units were made a tangled mass of wreckage by bombs which fell on them or near by. In one street buildings on both pavements were on fire, the flames meeting in the middle to form a bridge of flame.

## SEEN FROM DANISH COAST.

This was the night on which our pilots leaving the coast of Denmark saw Hull on fire. Whole streets were blocked with debris, preventing the passage of pumps ; others had great craters which brought the same delay ; people were trapped in buildings and had to be rescued by fire escapes ; the ground heaved under the explosion of the bombs, glass windows would grow red and then become molten ; walls crashed, roofs and ceilings fell in carrying more combustible material into the ground furnace, yet the firemen fought on. It was their business to save the City, and they did it by concentrating on keeping the fires in as confined a space as possible, thus preventing adjoining structures catching fire from sparks or flying embers.

It was a night of 464 outbreaks, almost all of a major character. The first began round about midnight ; at 8-36 a.m. the Regional Officer at Leeds was phoned : " All fires under control."

*One fact which should be stressed is that that night, at the height of the fires, the crew of the fire brigade petrol tanker went out with 750 gallons of petrol aboard, besides a considerable number of tins. Their job was to see that the water pumps had sufficient petrol to keep them working, and they did it. At one period the consumption reached 600 gallons an hour.*

Sometimes an odd fireman left his hose, or handed it to a mate, and went to the tank to fill a can ; sometimes soldiers helped, sometimes civilians. Often the cans had to be carried across heaps of rubble, round a street crater, over telephone and tram wires which tripped the carrier, sometimes through blazing buildings, *but not a single pump stopped for the sake of petrol as the motive power.*

Another memorable and gallant episode that night was that in which firemen climbed to the roofs of warehouses near the dockside and moving along the eaves kicked or threw hundreds of incendiaries to the ground.

In eight hours three members of the brigade were killed, five seriously injured and detained in hospital, and 22 attended medically but permitted to go home. Scores more received attention at their stations or at first aid posts for cuts, abrasions

SHATTERED INTERIOR OF RECKITT & COLMAN'S WORKS IN DANSOM LANE.

PAINT AND GUNPOWDER—SISSONS' BROS. WORKS AT STONEFERRY AFTER A HEAVY ATTACK.

and burns, but declined to add to the already overwhelming burdens of the hospital staffs.

## THE NEXT NIGHT.

The day was spent in checking and repairing equipment and surveying the basements of shops to see if the water there could be used that night in the event of a raid. In one instance 49,000 gallons were found, and in others lesser quantities. It was decided to leave it. The step proved a wise one.

Shortly after midnight the sirens sounded again, and it was quickly evident that the raid was to be on a similar scale to the previous one. This time, however, the target appeared to be concentrated on timber storage grounds, sawmills, silos and oil mills, though the centre of the City was not neglected. Early on, several telephone exchanges were damaged, and cables practically severed at points where they passed under the River Hull. Communication by telephone from one half of the City to the other was tenuous or impossible. Thus among other methods used, such as personal runners, use of observation posts, and the private lines of the L.N.E.R. signal boxes, a wireless scheme was put into operation. This was done with the assistance of the military.

Soon fires were reported from all areas, one notable one being at the premises of Messrs. Cornelius Parish, Ltd., Anlaby Road. While this was being fought under a rain of oil bombs, incendiaries and high explosives, a high wall collapsed killing four and injuring a number of firemen. That same night the Central Fire Station received direct hits on several occasions, three men being killed and a number injured.

## TERRIFIED ANIMALS RESCUED.

In the eastern area a fire at Messrs. Ranks flour mill had been quelled and the crew just leaving when a string of oil bombs and high explosives fell on the mill. It was soon obvious that the fire could not be stopped, so every effort was made to confine it, despite the fact that walls were falling and floors crashing in, while dust clouds of flour either blinded the firemen or made accurate observation impossible. The glare made the mill a target for the later bombers, and when a wall collapsed on the river side hundreds of tons of grain cascaded into the river.

It was in this area, and at this time, that a number of terrified horses were rescued from a blazing stable. They kicked and screamed in terror, but could not be moved until the rescuers placed bags over the heads of the horses. Even when led they insisted on walking over ground where an unexploded bomb had landed rather than face the glare coming from a row of burning shops!

It was the night that churches, theatres, picture palaces, mills, factories, hotels and tenement houses disappeared or became gaunt masses of blackened ruins, with dangerous walls which had to be pulled down. Altogether, 272 fires were attended, not so many as the previous night, but some of greater proportions.

Then began the day long task by desperately tired, hungry and dirty men of cleaning and sorting out equipment to be ready again. Happily, the need did not arise that night.

## WHEN RECKITT'S WAS ABLAZE.

From May 9th to July 18th, 1941, a number of raids produced 200 fires, the majority being on July 11th, when 187 were recorded.

DIRECT HIT IN JULY, 1941. SHATTERED PREMISES OF THE MIDLAND BANK IN WITHAM.

ANOTHER EAST HULL BANK—THIS TIME THAT OF THE HULL SAVINGS BANK.

Then on July 18th there came a raid which brought 89 fires. Early on a number of bombs fell in the vicinity of the main fire station, one which did not explode lodging itself in the roadway opposite, with the result that the station had to be evacuated of pumps and personnel except the control room staff. The bomb exploded at 8-30 in the morning.

One terrifying incident happened when a gas-holder was struck, and a huge sheet of flame ripped the sky. Happily there were no serious results, and the danger was over in a few minutes. There was a stick of bombs, too, on the works of Messrs. Reckitt & Colmån, Ltd. This caused a fire of major importance which did much damage. At the height of the fray a high and long wall collapsed, and though the firemen had very little warning of this possibility, they managed to get clear. For this blaze water was obtained from agricultural drains, but the water from the hoses soon had dyes, bath cubes, blacklead and disinfectants mixed with it. The effect, as the water ran into the sewers in the glare of the blaze, can be imagined.

## HOW GRAIN WAS SAVED.

The big fire of the night was that at Messrs. Spillers, Ltd., millers and grain merchants, in Cleveland Street. Here a bomb burst a large water main in the middle of the road, so water had to be relayed from the River Hull and also from a fire boat. A silo containing 35,000 tons of grain was the danger point. Large quantities of water would cause the grain to swell and burst the walls of the silo. If that happened and the grain fell into the River Hull navigation would be impeded or stopped. So it was decided to let the grain burn, but damp it down, and commence leading it away from the bottom of the silo. This was done, and the silo, with thousands of quarters of grain, invaluable to the country at that time, was saved.

That, in brief, and inadequately, is the story of the Hull Fire Services, for on August 18th, 1941, the National Fire Service came into operation, bringing unity of control and a similarity in methods of training and words of command, absent when each city or area had its own brigade. The turnover was somewhat difficult, for Hull was still the centre of attacks, but it was accomplished without any interference with the fire fighting service. For this fact thanks are due to a number of people and Corporation Departments in releasing valued employees to take over important administrative duties.

## PREPARED FOR V-BOMBS.

July 30th was the last of the big nights, but ease from fire fighting only meant that the men underwent training for other forms of warfare, notably for rescue work, should Hull come within the plans of the Germans for the reception of V-1 and V-2 bombs, then falling on the London area. Happily those precautions were never employed.

Thus ends a story of the Hull City Fire Brigade and men of the Auxiliary Force, who risked life and limb on countless occasions and accepted extreme physical exhaustion as something to be borne as best as possible until better times came. It would be unfair, however, to close without a tribute to those who attended to the administrative side, men and women who saw to the replacement of equipment from pins to pumps, kept the records, saw to the finances, arranged for food and hot drinks to be sent to fires ; in short, became responsible for seeing to every phase

God's Acres. Shell of Drypool Parish Church which, like many other Hull churches, suffered severely in the many raids.

of a fireman's service while he was hale, and looking after the affairs of his family when his duty became impossible for him to discharge. Nor must we omit acknowledgment of the help given by outside brigades, particularly those in the East Riding, always standing by during a warning, and always ready to come into the City the minute the call reached them.

Memory is a frail faculty, but no man or woman who lived in Hull during the war will ever forget the courage, endurance, and initiative of those who served in the Fire Brigade and saved the City from becoming first a cauldron, and then a land of blackened waste.

# BRAVE BOYS AND GIRLS

### THEIR MOTTO WAS " GET YOUR MESSAGE THROUGH "

All old soldiers know the perils faced by the company runner in the battlefield. No matter how fierce an artillery barrage might be the company runner had to try to get through with a message, using his own quick wit and initiative, for usually he was on his own, often on a lonely stretch, and if misfortune befell him then he had to tend his own wounds and struggle on—or perhaps die alone. Hence, company runners were selected for their intelligence, courage and sturdiness.

The Hull Civil Defence Service had at one time or another more than 2,000 such company runners, all volunteers, all boy and girl cyclists from 15 upwards. Their business was to be at danger points so that they could carry messages when ordinary methods of communication failed through enemy bombs destroying phone wires. Perhaps an ambulance was needed, perhaps a unit of the Fire Service. If so, they were brought, in spite of falling bombs, the blackness of the streets, the possibility of a tumble over the handlebars of the cycle into a shell crater that had not been there five minutes earlier. A message might have to be taken to the military authorities or bombed-out and frightened people guided to a reception centre. Incoming fire units, supply lorries and the like, driven by strangers to the City, had to be taken to the spot to which they had been directed.

NEVER FAILED.

All these things and many others were done by these boys and girls whose motto was " Get your message through." And in every case the message went through, though it meant that the messengers might be blown off their cycles by blast, find a road blocked and a wide detour necessary, or be faced with the need of lifting their machines on their shoulders and climbing over a mass of tangled girders mixed with bricks, masonry and broken glass which had once been a building.

It was gallant work, spoken of often and with something akin to awe by the people of Hull. It will be remembered with gratitude for years to come.

These young people had their baptism of battle when mere boys and girls, with no opportunity of training with veterans. Yet they never failed, never even faltered.

Before November, 1939, there was no Messenger Service except in the case of

THE PRESBYTERIAN CHURCH IN PROSPECT STREET.

FIREWATCHERS DIED UNDER THESE SMOULDERING RUINS OF GODDARD, WALKER & BROWN'S PREMISES IN QUEEN STREET.

some warden districts to which a few young people were attached. So, for all practical purposes, it was a new branch of Civil Defence. It had no traditions, no record to "live up to." The first volunteers and those who followed as vacancies were created through calling-up notices made the history.

When the "Alert" sounded those who were due for duty that night left their homes and went straight to action stations. There was no central rallying point for instructions. They went to every Warden Service District H.Q., to wardens' posts, rescue and casualty depots, first aid posts, report and control centres, W.V.S. head-quarters, rest centres, and district offices for after-raid work. In short, they went to every danger point, those allocated to the fire stations slinging their cycles on top of the fire engines and travelling with the crews in case reinforcements were required at the outbreak !

## SAVED POLICEMAN'S LIFE.

At one such incident on May 8th, 1941, a messenger, working with a 14-stone constable, saved the life of the latter by dragging him from a blazing garage to a wardens' post when the constable had been temporarily blinded by blast from a high explosive bomb. Then, through a hail of fire and explosives, he took a message to a first aid post. He found the post destroyed, so he cycled on to another centre for assistance. He finished the evening by rescuing people from the debris of a demolished house !

Perhaps this was an outstanding case, but letters to Cyclist Messenger H.Q. from people living in demolished areas reveal hundreds of instances where these boys and girls extinguished incendiary bombs, helped to fight fires, carried wounded to shelters, or did other deeds of a practical and humane character. Yet their place in the defence scheme was to carry messages !

Unfortunately, four were killed, one being a girl of but 18, the other two youths of 18 and a deputy divisional officer of 41. Four were wounded. Many cases are known where messengers stayed on duty though they had word that their own home had been demolished by bombs. One case is recorded of a district leader, "an inspiration to his fellow messengers," who stayed on duty for 72 hours. Many passed the Red Cross examination for first aid work as the result of studying at first aid posts while waiting orders to take a message.

## GAY, GALLANT COMPANY.

Even off duty these young people did not idle. They organised their own indoor and outdoor recreations, formed a band with 14 instruments and a mace, gathered fruit, flowers and vegetables from allotments and gardens for hospitals, and one Christmas made with their own hands more than 400 toys for children in hospitals. They raised £500 for the Lord Mayor's Air Raid Distress Fund through a series of social and other efforts, gave parties to poor children in their districts, giving up their own coupons to provide sweets for the guests, and finally had a dozen electric clocks installed in various hospitals.

Some think and others say that our young people are decadent !

The boys and girls forming the Hull Civil Defence Cyclist Messenger Corps made a gallant, gay and generous company, the services of which are remembered with respect and affection.

FIRE SERVICES DID HEROIC WORK WHEN BOMBERS SET HULL'S CITY CENTRE ALIGHT IN MAY, 1941.

STORY STREET BURNS AFTER THE BLITZ IN MAY, 1941.

## A JOB THAT WAS NOT EASY

### WORK OF THE BILLETING OFFICERS

Even people in distress like to have a say in where they are to go, though the accommodation be but temporary. Some want to know what the other people are like, the amount of privacy they are likely to have, what are the kitchen facilities, whether there is a bathroom, how convenient is the reception area regarding work, schools, churches and the like. The cynical might comment that beggars cannot be choosers, but bombed-out men and women are not beggars. They have their pride.

Hence, a little imagination will conjure up some of the difficulties met with and overcome by the billeting officers of the Hull Corporation. For a time men and women in various services undertook the duties in addition to their ordinary work, but in July, 1941, 22 new officers took up duty, their predecessors being retained as emergency officers.

Altogether, 51,087 homeless people were accommodated until such time as they made arrangements with relatives and friends, or found their own lodgings. It says much for the good will of Hull people, and the tact of the officers, that only on a few occasions was the Register of Billets used. In no case were compulsory billeting powers used.

Billeting did not consist merely of taking a person or a family to a house and introducing the parties. A line of approach had to be found and used, the needs and desires of billeter and billetee accommodated, records maintained, payments made, contact kept with the newcomers and, in several hundred cases, travel vouchers issued, following preliminary inquiries.

People who left the City night after night during the heavy bombing, to roam the countryside and rest where they might, were interrogated and records taken. This resulted in special accommodation being found for them on the outskirts of the City.

Another phase of this work was to find lodgings for thousands of building trade men drafted to the City to carry out repairs to houses. It was not always easy, for many of these men were of an independent nature and did not like being sent to Hull, but it was accomplished.

## ELECTRICITY

It is common knowledge that in these days electricity is the main source of power for industry and domestic life in every large community. In Kingston upon Hull the Corporation Electricity Department, in 1939, supplied an area of 162 square miles, with a population of about 400,000, and was connected to the grid to which it usually exported energy. In built-up areas every street had one or more cables, and there were sub-stations at various points according to the density of the population. Hence any bomb falling into a built-up area was likely to damage part of the system.

What happened? Some 25 high explosive bombs fell within half a mile of the power station, and eight within 200 yards of the engine room. Some cables were cut in every one of the 80 raids. The equipment in countless factories and private houses was damaged, the Department's own administrative offices or workshops were

Shop premises in Beverley Road reduced to a pile of rubble by high explosives.

Shattered masonry of Hull's G.P.O. falls across Alfred Gelder Street.

sufficiently damaged to impede service, yet the supply to the City as a whole never failed. Generally speaking, no large consumer and very few small ones were ready to take supply again before it was available for them.

This was not due to good luck, but solely to good management, sound preparation, and unswerving loyalty on the part of the staff from the highest to the lowest grade.

The meaning of the plan was completed in September, 1938, materials purchased and laid by as reserves for emergency, shelters erected, and vulnerable machinery and sub-stations given splinter and blast protection. In all, 81 buildings were thus protected. Staff dispersal stations were arranged, and electrically-operated sirens connected up and serviced. Then, when the public shelter system was launched, large scale heating and lighting was installed in the shelters. All these were accomplished in addition to the normal work falling to the Department.

When the raids themselves came the members of the staff found the facilities and time to sterilise the blankets of trekkers to outlying areas, man a public shelter underneath the main showrooms to which sometimes as many as 300 people flocked, and provide for the W.V.S. a high power industrial vacuum cleaner with two suction hoses large enough and strong enough to absorb pulverised glass, soot and plaster from two houses at a time. It thus became possible to make at least one room of a house in a badly damaged district habitable in quick time.

It is easy to imagine the strain on the staff consequent on the inspection and repairs of the cables, sometimes in awkward positions, their private family anxieties, and the ever-present possibility of a general breakdown. Happily the latter never happened, though on one occasion this came very near. A stick of bombs which fell within 150 yards of the engine room on the night of March 18th-19th, 1941, cut through the cables connecting the station to the grid. Only one turbo-alternator was running, and the shock of the fault on the cables caused the machine to so surge in speed that it became unstable. Despite the bombing and the fact that the station seemed to be the target for the night, the engineers in charge took suitable controlling action and the system came safely through.

While tribute is due to the power station operating staff, working as the men did through continuous shifts regardless of expectations and realisations (and it has to be remembered that the strain of the first was often worse than the second), the greatest stress from raids fell upon the Distribution Engineer and his staff. As mentioned earlier, some cables were cut in every raid, and over the whole period the equivalent of every main trunk cable was at one time or another out of service for a short time due to bombing. This entailed inspection by engineers during the alerts, and long hours of rectification work after the all clear.

This would, of course, have been impossible of the members of the staff at the Report Centre, and those at the central control point of the Electricity Department housed in a surface shelter at the power station.

On top of all this, the Department formed its own unit of the L.D.V. in June, 1940, with the General Manager, despite his other grave responsibilities as its Commanding Officer.

Only those directly associated with the electricity industry will be able to realise all the technical difficulties involved. Hull men and women in other callings, and whose livelihood as well as domestic supplies depends on an uninterrupted supply of electricity, had need to be—and indeed were—grateful for this blessing during the raids. This result was due in equal measure to planning, administration, efficiency,

GRAIN AND DEBRIS POUR INTO THE OLD HARBOUR AFTER THE COMPLETE DESTRUCTION OF RANK'S FLOUR MILLS.

ANOTHER FLOUR MILL IS HIT. MESSRS. SPILLERS' PREMISES. AUGUST, 1941.

and, above all, intense loyalty on the part of men and women of all grades and all sections of the Department, whether engineers, telephonists, maintenance men, clerks, or those engaged on the reconditioning of domestic installations, ovens, kettles and the like. These latter might seem minor things when the ordeal of Hull is looked on as a whole. They were mighty important at the time to the woman wishing to provide a meal for her man and her family.

How serious air raid damage was to the Department can be gleaned from the fact that up to the end of the serious raiding it was estimated as costing £120,000, and that without the nerve centre of the supply having a direct hit.

## THE MAINTENANCE OF GAS SUPPLIES

The supply of gas for both industrial and household use ranks as one of the highest public services in Hull. In peace-time there are all manner of hazards to contend with, for though a useful servant, gas is a bad master, indeed, a highly dangerous one. Yet though 493 mains belonging to the British Gas Light Co., which serves more than half the City, were smashed in bomb-scarred roads, and 3,326 service pipes in buildings were damaged, the situation never got so far out of hand that the service was wholly interrupted for more than a few days. That was not just luck, but was a result of planning and unceasing labour in time of emergency.

At the outbreak of war a large reserve stock of mains, valves, repair gear, tools and equipment was built up. Valves were inserted in the district mains, and alterations were carried out that enabled the City to be divided into 14 areas, each of which could be isolated. The value of these preparations was proved time after time when, though some districts were without a supply at all, people not far away had some sort of a service.

There were occasions, however, when everything had to be cut off at headquarters; this was done on the night of March 18th, 1941, for the first time since the British Gas Light Company began to operate 120 years ago. The decision was taken because of damage to a manufacturing plant, but the supply was restored on March 22nd. The same step was repeated on the morning of May 8th, the stoppage this time lasting until the 13th. Then, on July 18th, there was another total stoppage, the service being partially restored the next day, and wholly on the 22nd. For the rest, the stoppages were of a district character.

### KNOWN TO PILOTS.

There is no doubt that the whereabouts of the gasworks were known to the enemy pilots, for the premises were the target for 39 H.E. bombs as well as countless incendiaries. One H.E. fell plump on the second largest gas holder on the premises and destroyed it in a minute. The holder had contained about two million cubic feet of gas, sufficient to supply the whole City for 24 hours. The official report of the occurrence is something of an understatement, since it records merely that " there was a huge beacon hundreds of feet high." It goes on that : " Due to arrangements made beforehand to shut off manufacture if necessary, this holder fire was extinguished by the staff within a very short time, preventing a target for following bombers."

On another occasion a direct hit on a shelter from a H.E. bomb flung a part

The C.W.S. Mill in Cumberland Street—destroyed in 1941.

Harley Street Corner.

of the structure through the air and planted it on the crown of a gasholder 130 yards away.

The staff knew well enough that they were working in a highly dangerous zone with a highly dangerous element which might be the source of unending fires and explosions. Yet there was no faltering. They had to find the source of escape. This meant working in the dark and in soil turned to clay and slushy mud, for often when water mains and gas were smashed together an enormous amount of water flooded the gas mains and wide areas round about.

DEVOTION TO DUTY.

It was fitting, therefore, that the mains foreman, as representative of the repair gangs, should be awarded the British Empire Medal for devotion to duty.

As to the headquarters and works staffs, it says much for them that only on three occasions was the supply completely cut off, in spite of the fact that the manufacture of gas is a continuous process. Raid or no raid, the filling of coal into retort settings, the discharge of coke, the attention to machinery, boilers, benzole, and concentrated ammonia plants have to go on.

Works managers, householders, proprietors of hotels and restaurants, to say nothing of barbers, were certainly inconvenienced on odd occasions by the absence of supplies. What might have happened to them and the City as a whole except for the skill and loyalty shown by so many at headquarters is beyond the scope of the imagination of the average man.

## THE TELEPHONE DEPARTMENT

Telephoning is a prosaic sort of business, but even in peace one cannot telephone without the equipment being maintained in first-class condition. Add to this knowledge the fact that the Naval, Military and Civil Defence Services used 4,000 instruments in the Hull area when bombs were causing constant breaks and disruptions and one has an idea of the task which faced the Hull Telephone Department from 1939 to 1945. It was, of course, imperative that a line of communication other than manual be maintained, for even though a reserve of men, women, boys and pigeons was maintained, speedy contact with anti-aircraft batteries and out-of-town authorities was essential. To do this the staff was called upon on many occasions when the risk of death or injury was very great.

To save time it was the practice for all members to report for duty at the exchange nearest their homes immediately after the " All Clear." Thus the men were enabled to repair lines in their immediate neighbourhood almost at once. The first test came on March 31st, 1941, when the Civil Defence headquarters in the heart of the City were destroyed, for it became necessary for a new service to be installed at another address immediately. Thus came evidence of the wisdom and foresight of having stocks of apparatus in several buildings, for even though a building nearest the destroyed C.D. headquarters had been badly damaged, sufficient equipment was found and made ready for work by daylight the following morning. A job like this was, of course, on a large scale, but individually the call was even more tense, for approximately 2,000 subscribers' instruments and 81 switchboards in business houses were totally destroyed. That replacement was the responsibility of the inside department. For their part the outside men had to replace no fewer than 94 lengths of underground cables varying in size from 80 to 100 yards in length, come weather, warning, or raid itself in daylight or darkness. One of their most difficult replacements was in Anne Street, but the same night it was again damaged and a water main burst so that heavy flooding had to be contended with. This during a period when both material and man power was at a premium, beside the fact that the men employed had their natural anxieties about their homes and families. On top of this, about the same period, a cable in Clarence Street, serving a very congested area, was damaged so that at the same time no fewer than 4,000 lines were out of order. The strain was such that it became physically impossible for the permanent staff to cope with the work and generous recognition is made of the assistance offered (and accepted) by the General Post Office and the Beverley Corporation. Personal dangers, too, had to be contended underground, in the way of craters and shell holes, and overhead in the clearance of broken wires. Justice also demands that tribute be paid to the courage and tenacity of the indoor staff in remaining at their posts, particularly at night. One example of this courage was found when a high explosive bomb fell at an exchange within 20 yards of the emergency board in use at that time. So serious was the situation at one period that communication out of the City was totally cut except for one line which linked Hull with Leeds, and that had to serve the Military, Civil Defence, Police and National Fire Service. Only those in residence in Hull at that time can realise the intense strain enveloping, and, indeed, overwhelming those engaged in the Telephone Service whether in a major or minor capacity at the time.

The thanks of Hull are most certainly due to the staff of the Hull Corporation Telephones Department for the courage, efficiency and courtesy shown in maintaining vital lines of communication, both in and out of Hull, for with the exception of London, no centre of population experienced such a lengthy test of loyalty and ability, whether the latter consisted of jointing outside apparatus or linking up subscribers, many of whom showed often enough signs of impatience under the stress and uncertainty which was part of the price which had to be paid for living in Hull from 1940 to 1945.

## THE TRANSPORT DEPARTMENT

The first comment to make regarding the Hull Transport's staff is that the men were the first in the country to indicate their willingness to work throughout the services during the alert periods until the " danger " signal was imminent. This fact and the knowledge that the services continued to operate during the most severe raids had a remarkable effect on the spirit and morale of the public. In view of Hull's geographical position, and the especial need for an intense blackout in all main roads and all vehicles, public and private, this was a notable step both in courage and example. Some dislocation was, of course, bound to occur, especially after the very heavy raids of May and July, 1941, but this never lasted for any length of time and thus throughout the war the men and women on all public transport, both Corporation or otherwise publicly owned, and running well out into the suburbs, won the admiration and thanks of the people.

It has to be remembered that the crews, both at the front and the rear of the

## HOMES OF THE PEOPLE

Homes of the People, as they were left night after night by Hitler's raiders.

Bathtub Salvage from wrecked homes in the Garden Village area.

# HOMES OF THE PEOPLE

North Hull Housing Estate.

Buckingham Street.

# HOMES OF THE PEOPLE

RESCUE SQUADS BUSY ON DEMOLISHED PROPERTY IN BUCKINGHAM STREET.

BEAN STREET.

# HOMES OF THE PEOPLE

East Hull Housing Estate.

A bomb crater in James Reckitt Avenue.

vehicles, had to work in an intense darkness, often miles from their own neighbourhood, with consequent difficulty in getting home through the street rubble, and all the anxiety over the welfare of their families during the raids while the operators were at work.

The raids of May and July certainly meant interruptions, but there was never a complete hold-up. Buses were diverted to side streets to avoid craters and unexploded bombs, short journeys were operated on both buses and trams because of damage and destruction of overhead equipment. Shuttle bus services were instituted, notices of changed services had to be chalked up on notice boards, buildings, and on the pavements. Buses had to be borrowed from other Corporations and other operators. Arrangements had to be made for the feeding and sleeping of the crews, evacuation of women and children, the aged and infirm had to be carried, and in some instances vehicles withdrawn from regular routes, but in spite of all handicaps public transport was maintained, summer and winter alike, from before dawn to after dark, on strange routes, damaged highways and with the minimum of lights, but almost always with courtesy and consideration for harassed timid passengers with nerves on edge.

If the people of Hull ever forget or fail to appreciate the mountainous trouble overcome by the men and women of the Transport Services during 1939-1944 then they should cry shame on themselves.

Apart from the ordinary passenger services, the Department was responsible for the importation of workmen from the West Riding to deal with raid damage, with their feeding and billeting miles away, an added difficulty being the dispersal of the buses following the destruction of so many vehicles in May, 1941. Regular members of the staff stood by for the mobile canteens, the removal of homeless to rest centres after heavy raids, the removal of trekkers, especially the East Hull area, and generally working in and not away from the centres of danger and destruction.

Of the material damage it is sufficient to record that overhead equipment on both tram and trolley bus routes as well as ground equipment, losses were sustained on many occasions. Over 9 miles of wire and 38 traction poles were erected during the raid period, the staff often having to work night and day to provide equipment for quick resumption of the services essential to the public.

In addition the main administrative offices were destroyed during a raid in May, 1941, all records and office equipment being lost. Then the traffic office was destroyed in a further raid. Those losses were sufficient to cripple any traffic service apart from the trials and losses mentioned earlier, but the Transport men and women of Hull retained their sanity, their ability and their courtesy, thus enabling the citizens to uphold their own sense of proportion during the trials which almost nearly, but not quite, drove them crazy.

# WATER SUPPLIES

The Water Department commenced its war-time preparations early in 1938 and by the outbreak of hostilities had built up an organisation which, together with the purchase of necessary plant and equipment, proved satisfactory in meeting all requirements of the war period. In fact, no alteration was required to the organisation and no additional plant or material was purchased during the period.

High Street. One of the City's oldest thoroughfares.

House topples almost into the drain on Cottingham Road.

The total population dependent upon the Undertaking was approximately 400,000 within an area of 310 square miles. The total length of pipe networks was approximately 750 miles with mains varying between 2 in. and 30 in. diameter.

It will be appreciated that water is the community's primary necessity and is required to be available under all conditions. Furthermore, water is the main weapon against fire. In addition, it was envisaged that bombs damaging water mains may cause similar damage to sewers, and there would be the very serious danger of pollution of water supplies unless rapid isolation and effective sterilisation were carried out.

Due to Hull's geographical position, it was realised that little or no warning of air raids might be forthcoming. In view of the city's isolation from other large water authorities, it was anticipated that no immediate help would be available, and, therefore, the war-time organisation was based on the assumption that the Hull Water Undertaking would have to be self-supporting.

One of the main points of the organisation was dispersal, and it was decided that the control of the Undertaking should be transferred from Alfred Gelder Street to the Cottingham Pumping Station some 5 miles distant from the city centre. Special private telephone lines were installed from this Control to the main pumping stations and depots, so that should the telephone service go out of operation the Water Undertaking would still be able to maintain communication within its own Department.

Although the Central Depot in Clough Road combined all facilities for accommodation of repair gangs, decontamination squads, etc., it was considered a vulnerable area and was also de-centralised as much as possible by the formation of fully equipped sub-depots at various points within the area.

The main-laying and distribution section employees were fully trained in their respective tasks under assumed war conditions, and training reached a stage when personnel were able to work for three-hour stretches wearing full anti-gas equipment.

With the entire water supply being dependent on pumping machinery, it was considered essential to guard against the possibility of any of the pumping stations being put out of action, and this provision was met by the purchase of two portable pumping sets, each set being capable of pumping 5,000,000 gallons a day, if necessary, directly from shafts on the lines of adits. Similarly, Diesel sets were obtained as stand-bys for the booster pumping stations supplying the outside areas.

It was realised that bombing would cause serious damage to the trunk main system, upon which the whole of the City's water pressure depends. To overcome this contingency, two 1,000 gallons per minute petrol-driven booster pumps were purchased, their use being to bridge the gaps caused by large craters or obstruction caused by debris, and to restore as quickly as possible the water supply before any major repairs or clearances were made.

One of the most difficult tasks in the isolation of damaged large mains was the manual operation of the large valves, which, if required to be carried out in anti-gas equipment would have virtually become a physical impossibility. To overcome this difficulty, the Department successfully devised a petrol-driven headstock for the rapid operation of these large valves, thus making it possible to quickly isolate any damaged section.

As a means of providing for the domestic supply in any badly bombed area, eight lorries each carrying 600-gallon tanks and fitted with special draw-off taps were

BEDROOM SCENE AFTER GERMAN RAIDERS HAD DESTROYED ANOTHER OF HULL'S LITTLE HOMES.

HOMES OF REST WERE NOT EXCLUDED. HERE ARE TRINITY ALMSHOUSES IN ANLABY ROAD SHATTERED IN A NIGHT RAID.

made available for instant use, and many additional tanks were held in reserve. Further, 50 special standpipes, each having four draw-off taps were also provided for fixing to the nearest hydrant at which water was available. Cross-connections were also made between various trunk mains within the area, thus giving a quick alternative supply route in cases of emergency.

It was also recommended that the numerous agricultural drains in the area could be utilised for fire-fighting purposes. The Department suggested that as these drains were tidal, manually-operated sluice gates could be erected at the outfalls and thus maintain a constant water level in the drains. The necessary gates were designed, constructed and operated by the Water Department until March, 1940, when the control was handed over to the Fire Service.

On the Water Department rested the responsibility of maintaining the purity of the water supply under all conditions, and as damaged mains were liable to pollution by broken sewers it was very necessary that damaged sections were sterilised effectively. At no time during the aftermath of the heaviest raids did the Department's repair squads fail to carry out this very important duty, and due to their efficiency no water-borne epidemic was experienced.

The following particulars will give some idea of the extent of damage sustained by the Undertaking during hostilities.

A total of 394 mains were severed, the diameters varying from 3 in. to 30 in., the aggregate length requiring replacement being $3\frac{1}{4}$ miles.

Reference might be made in particular to damage sustained in the heavy air raids during May and July, 1941. In the heavy attack in May, 118 mains were damaged in two successive nights, and 72 in the July raid. During the latter raid, a large proportion of the damage inflicted was to trunk mains, and this was the only occasion that a call had to be made for outside help. In this respect, the assistance given by the employees of the Goole Water Department who worked in Hull for as long as 14 to 16 hours per day for three to four weeks to effect the necessary repairs is recorded with appreciation.

Even after the heaviest raids, a water supply was always available to domestic users, although it was occasionally necessary to utilise the mobile tankers and bring into use the hydrant standpipes.

The Undertaking also received extensive structural damage to its buildings. A land mine and several high explosive bombs fell within 300 yards of the Dunswell Pumping Station. High explosives and incendiaries fell within the precincts of the Cottingham Pumping Station, and several land mines fell close by. Numerous H.E. bombs were dropped near the Bilton and Springhead Pumping Stations, the latter being extensively damaged by a " flying bomb " in December, 1944.

The Keldgate Reservoir was straddled by a stick of five bombs, but only one pierced the roof and, fortunately, failed to explode. Bombs also fell within the Central Depot causing considerable damage to a large part of the covered warehouse and the Department's houses nearby. Bomb detonations in the vicinity of the Hornsea and Withernsea water towers shook the foundations to such an extent that cracks appeared in the water-retaining parts of the structures, and, as a consequence, extensive repairs were necessary.

Despite the damage described above, it is of particular note that no serious interruption of the water supply was experienced, and this was due solely to the dogged determination of the personnel and their constant loyalty in carrying out their arduous

Mobile Canteens run by the W.V.S. and other organisations did fine work in feeding the bombed-out people of the City.

This First Aid Post on Hessle Road had a direct hit.

duties. No matter how good an organisation may be, it cannot be effective unless supported by the personnel performing their required tasks.

The Department may lay claim to a high place amongst its " blitzed " contemporaries, for the water supply was always maintained and, consequently, never made a " Head-line Story " of distress. The Undertaking thus preserved its anonymity to the end, surely a true test of achievement.

# EVACUATION

The vitally important business of evacuation was entrusted to the Education Department. To realise the tremendous scope of this problem one has to remember that plans had to be prepared for the movement of approximately 35,000 children of school age ; in addition the aged, crippled, the feeble, and the blind, expectant mothers and the none-too-intelligent had to be catered for in organised parties, all in a matter of three days in the event of immediate urgency. The first hint from the Government came in January, 1939, and planning commenced immediately.

The generous support of head masters and mistresses was at once forthcoming, and as time passed with the possibilities and probabilities arising generous co-operation was received from teachers of all ages, some settled in life and on the point of retirement, others just out of college and in the full bloom of vigorous life.

Amongst the problems to be decided at an early stage were the areas in East Riding and North Lincolnshire to which the parties had to go. Homes, hostels, schooling facilities, assembly points, supervisors and leaders, buses and trains had to be arranged. Moreover, it should be remembered that there was no precedent for such a procedure. There was no compulsion, no regimentation in operation, everything depended on the good will and co-operation of the organisers and the organised.

With the co-operation of the Hull Transport Department, buses met the parties at a pre-arranged time at the various schools named as assembly points to convey them to the Hull central railway station, a nearby station, or perhaps straight to the reception area. An idea of the transport involved can be envisaged from the fact that approximately 100 special trains were arranged for and provided.

The Government instructions for the plan to be put into operation were received on the morning of August 31st, 1939, the evacuation date being fixed for the following day, Friday, September 1st. These instructions were passed to those concerned during the Thursday afternoon and the evacuation commenced on the Friday. The first day saw the departure of the main body of school children with their teachers. None were told the destination and an appeal was made to parents to stay away from the railway stations in order to avoid spoiling the spirit of adventure which had been inculcated into the children. On the second day mothers with children of pre-school age together with expectant mothers and evacuees in other categories were moved out of the environments of the City. The third day, Sunday, September 3rd, the day on which war on Germany was formally declared, saw the departure of the remainder available to go if they were wishful and willing.

Unfortunately, very many weakened.

CLOUDS OF WAR HANG OVER CENTRAL HULL, ABLAZE AFTER THE FIRST BIG FIRE BLITZ OF MAY, 1941.

THIS ONE DID NOT GO OFF !!! A PARACHUTE MINE FALLS IN THE GARDEN OF AN EAST HULL HOME.

Records show that though preparations were made and facilities provided for the evacuation of approximately 100,000 people, only 30,632 children and adults took advantage of the facilities. Time proved that in the case of parents the fatalistic view that " we live or die together " predominated, while to many adults the lure of home comforts, neighbours and the corner shop proved too magnetic.

In view of this poor response the Government arranged for another evacuation of school children on September 8th, which resulted in a further 2,260 children moving. Even though the number did not reach the total planned and hoped for, the magnitude of the undertaking can be envisaged when it is remembered that all had to be ticketed, transported, fed and bedded.

The absence of any immediate bombing meant that there was a gradual and growing number who returned, with the result that there were numerous children left to run wild in the City since the schools were closed for fear of a major catastrophe by the dropping of a bomb on a building full of pupils.

In the latter part of 1940, following the heavy air raids on Coventry, plans were prepared for the evacuation of any homeless in Hull should the port be the victim of a similar outrage. Again the task was left to the Director of Education to prepare the scheme. Administrative headquarters and sub-stations were arranged and the co-operation of the teaching staff again offered and accepted. There were ten such divisions. How wise and effective were the plans made and administered was more than proved in the tragedies which followed the vicious attacks in May, 1941. The effects of the blitz of May 7th-8th, 1941, were so severe that the Emergency Committee decided that modifications of the original evacuation scheme were necessary and the outcome was that in the few days between May 9th and 11th, 1941, a total of 8,255 people were evacuated.

Damage to property necessitated a scheme for the evacuation of homeless people, this coming into operation in May, 1941. No fewer than 1,451 teachers volunteered for this task, while 50 members of the educational administrative staff were seconded for duty for the same purpose. Schools were allocated as reception centres for registration, etc. These were manned by teacher volunteers who also acted as liaison officers with reception areas, travelling guides, and discharged the manifold duties which arose. In three nights they moved 627 persons from wrecked homes to safer quarters. Then in August came instructions to prepare for the evacuation of mothers with children under five, an intensive publicity campaign being launched, the pulpit, poster and wireless all being used. In addition, opportunity was offered individuals to make private arrangements under the official scheme, the evacuation officials being authorised to issue the necessary certificates, travel warrants and the like to those involved. The number taking advantage of this totalled more than 30,000.

Then followed the problem of providing clothing and footwear for very poor children, £11,000 being expended in a brief period and though provision was made for the recovery of money from the parents according to their financial standing, the purchase, transport and fitting of such garments was a major task. In addition, the Authority had to make arrangements for the transfer of pupils of secondary schools, those devoted to special trades, and those caring for the afflicted such as deaf, blind, or crippled. Some schools went as complete units, while others had to carry out their educational programme as efficiently as circumstances permitted, though the classes were, in some cases, miles apart.

CAR FOR SALE, BUT NOT IN VERY GOOD CONDITION, AFTER A COTTINGHAM ROAD BOMB.

"BUSINESS AS USUAL IN A NORTH-EAST COAST TOWN," SAID THE CAPTION TO THIS PICTURE WHEN IT WAS PUBLISHED DURING THE WAR.

SUMMARY.

The following is a summary of the number of persons evacuated under organised and private arrangements within the official scheme following its inception in September, 1939.

*Under Organised Arrangements :*
| | |
|---|---:|
| Unaccompanied School Children | 31,038 |
| Mothers and Children : (a) Mothers | 5,240 |
| (b) Children | 9,737 |
| Expectant Mothers | 2,827 |
| Other Classes, *e.g.* Aged, Infirm, Crippled, Blind | 3,562 |

*Under Private Arrangements within the Official Scheme :*
| | |
|---|---:|
| Unaccompanied Children | 6,750 |
| Mothers and Children : (a) Mothers | 7,832 |
| (b) Children | 13,788 |
| Expectant Mothers | 300 |
| Other Classes, *e.g.* Aged, Infirm, Crippled, Blind | 2,501 |
| *Homeless Persons* | 8,882 |
| TOTAL | 92,457 |

The evacuation of people not essential or even necessary to the welfare and trade of the port during wartime was a Herculean task. Many were unwilling to go and many too eager to return, despite appeals, offers, inducements, and warnings of danger ahead. At times the difficulties appeared almost overwhelming through lack of co-operation on the part of those whose safety was the Authority's first concern. How many lives were saved and how many bodies remained healthy and whole instead of crippled and useless no man can tell. That the Education Authority, however, rendered a distinct and valuable service in the defence of Hull during wartime is beyond all question and merits the outstanding thanks of the present and future generations.

# 86,715 HOUSES DAMAGED

IN September, 1939, Hull had 92,660 houses of varying sizes and values, but all capable of accommodating families. In the course of the war

> 1,472 were totally destroyed,
> 2,882 so badly damaged that demolition may be necessary,
> 3,789 needed repairs beyond the scope of first aid,
> 11,589 were seriously damaged, but patched up,
> 66,983 were slightly damaged, a total of
>
> 86,715.

These figures show that only 5,945 houses escaped damage in any form. Some of the 86,715 were struck more than once, in some instances twice and thrice, so that altogether 146,915 individual damages were sustained. The business of repairing

Rubble Search by Rescue Squads who put in long hours of arduous duty.

Drink for Fido, an incident symbolic of the humanity which survived all that Nazi raiders could do.

them, either direct or through a contractor, fell within the scope of the City Architect's Department.

On one night alone, that of December 20th, 1942, no fewer than 1,064 houses were damaged. The whole of them, excepting those classified for evacuation, were made wind and weatherproof before Christmas, a period when we have the shortest spell of daylight. Night work, of course, was impossible owing to the black-out.

The system adopted was that at 7-30 each morning after a raid selected men visited the stricken areas. They decided whether the damaged houses should be patched up, repaired temporarily or permanently, or evacuated. The information was circulated to the competent Air Raid Welfare Department in a matter of a few hours (10 a.m. was the hour aimed at) so that the departments could plan their schemes of accommodation, food and the like. The City was divided into areas with so many building contractors allocated to each area. Hence, the contractors were on the spot. During the intense raiding periods they were never off it.

## " HELP YOURSELF " SCHEME.

On some occasions it was necessary to operate a " Help Yourself " Scheme devised by the City Architect. Under this scheme dumps of material were placed at given points under the care of a competent foreman. Householders willing to make their homes weatherproof reported the size of the window blown in, or of the gap in the roof, and had the necessary paper, felt, etc., cut out for them. In addition, they were supplied with laths and nails, all free. In many cases this meant a patchwork job, but the wind and rain were kept out, and in addition, the family was able to have a light indoors when darkness fell.

In due time, of course, all work was overhauled and brought up to the Ministry of Health standards.

In addition to the above invaluable contribution to the welfare of shocked and desolate people, the City Architect's Department had the responsibility of adapting buildings as first aid posts, strengthening hospitals, and equipping them with shelters, erecting cleansing stations, and building mortuaries, sand-bagging and making alterations to police stations, converting houses into sick bays, protecting plant and equipment at telephone exchanges, requisitioning houses, erecting 700 external air raid shelters at schools, even converting a building into a home for dogs and domestic pets taken from damaged property or found wandering.

The schools alone called for 18,500 maintenance orders and 6,000 reports in the five years.

# SHELTERS

## PROVISION COST £1,500,000

It can be imagined that the provision of shelters for the people was an important and early consideration of the members of the City Council. The business was left to the Workshops Section of the City Engineer's Department, and following the crisis of Munich in September, 1938, some 5,500 domestic shelters were erected, or partially so, and 68 communal trench shelters in the heart of the City. Then the order to cease work came, but even so sites continued to be inspected and laid out,

CUP OF TEA AND A GASPER FOR A FIRST AID WORKER AT A MOBILE CANTEEN.

GRIMY, BUT UNDEFEATED, CIVIL DEFENCE WORKERS TAKE A BREATHER AT ONE OF THE MOBILE CANTEENS RUN BY THE W.V.S.

with the result that within seven weeks of the outbreak of war 1,100 temporary timber sandbagged shelters capable of accommodating 40,000 were completed. By December, 1939, also, 700 domestic shelters a week were being constructed.

Then came time for the construction of brick and concrete buildings of a communal character, for private houses, for hospitals, schools, wardens' posts, trekkers to the country, etc., as well as the strengthening and shoring up to safety pitch of basements in large buildings. We will save time and space by giving the details of the cover provided against blast and splinter :

| | | |
|---|---|---|
| Communal and Public Shelters | 2,698 | to hold 124,454 |
| Steel Shelters (Anderson) . | 15,583 | |
| Domestic Surface . . . | 21,095 | ,, 146,712 |
| Indoor Shelters (delivered) . | 1,985 | ,, 5,013 |

The volume of the job can be realised when it is stated that the above figures do not include the provision for those engaged in Civil Defence work, and that in due time the shelters were bunked, or at least provided with seating accommodation, heated and lighted. The total cost was £1,500,000. The number of lives saved was full reward for the tremendous personal effort and labour in haulage and man power, and justified the cost, huge as it was.

## ALMOST A MIRACLE

On the night of May 7th-8th, 1941, the basement of a five-storey factory held 927 people. Two parachute mines dropped, one on the east side of the shelter, the other on the west. Then a large calibre H.E. bomb fell on the roof of the building. Yet the only casualty was that of a Merchant Navy man, who went home to change his slippers for boots and was killed outside his own house by blast.

## A SHELTER HIT

The tragedy in Holderness Road, when a public shelter in Ellis Terrace was hit, was on April 16th, 1941. A parachute mine made a direct hit, every occupant in the shelter being killed. It is estimated that the number was 60. Five hundred people in the vicinity were rendered homeless.

# WELFARE

It can be imagined that welfare work played an important part in the life of a bombed city, and by welfare is meant not merely the promiscuous giving out of gifts from clothing to sweets, but a planned scheme which saw to the immediate wants of those affected, and—equally important—maintained their morale by practical advice and assistance for some time. People who had lost their homes wholly or partly were not fobbed off with something to keep them quiet, but kept in touch with as long as necessary, and their legitimate claims on the Government or Local Authority seen to.

Thus various organisations, to be named later, were, for the purpose of administration, linked up with one central body. Between them they established District Offices in a place near where a raid had occurred, for preliminary inquiry into the affairs of those who had lost goods, but were able to look after their affairs ;

N.F.S. MEN ATTACK ONE OF THE BUILDINGS LEFT ABLAZE BY NAZI BOMBERS.

" WE CAN TAKE IT "—THUMBS UP AND A CHEERY SMILE BEHIND THE SHATTERED WINDOWS OF A HULL HOME.

established reception centres where the displaced people could find temporary shelter and be given hot drinks pending the finding of permanent accommodation ; provided permanent reception centres and hostels ; administered the Lord Mayor's Air Raid Distress Fund ; provided transport for those who desired to spend the night on the outskirts of the City ; salvaged and stored household goods until the owner could find a new place ; maintained a register and an information bureau whereby those killed or wounded could be traced by relatives ; founded and staffed sick bays ; saw to the furnishing of empty houses where families could gather together again until affairs could be straightened out.

Bringing all these organisations under one head, yet leaving them to attend their own particular branch, necessitated complete co-operation. Following an " Alert," an officer from each unit attended headquarters, the incidents were plotted on the map, and the information available despatched to the various centres.

Thus the officers responsible for reception centres, hostels and emergency feeding set their machines going. Canteens were sent to bombed centres as soon as practicable, blankets and clothing taken in a van or by other means ; the Food Officer arranged for the early replacements of stocks in districts where food shops had been destroyed. District offices for immediate relief were selected. Nor was there anything spasmodic about the service, for a 24-hour day and night roster was maintained, raid or no raid. Nor were there any hard and fast regulations. Officials and volunteers were given guidance, but they were also given authority to act as they thought best under the circumstances.

Never at any time was the relief afforded identified with the Poor Law.

The scheme was evolved nine months before the outbreak of war, and so careful was the planning that it was never altered fundamentally—only extended. Indeed, after the start of the war it was adopted by the Government as a basis for other cities to work on.

Now, in the brief space available, let us see what happened.

## RECEPTION CENTRES.

Church, chapel and mission halls were marked for reception centres, on which the bombed-out could concentrate for cover. Auxiliary lighting, heat, water and sanitation were installed, soap, brushes, palliases, and blankets provided. It was considered inadvisable to have too many distressed people in one centre, so the centres were classified as first, second and third, with certain schools as shadow centres. The scheme was administered by the Women's Voluntary Services, and so excellent were the arrangements that when the H.Q. of this organisation was put out of action by an outsize bomb on March 31st, 1941, the scheme functioned without a hitch.

This efficiency is shown in the fact that on the night of the heaviest raid, May 7th, 1941, out of 7,350 people using the reception centres all but 400 were accommodated elsewhere the following day, making room for another 7,000 on the night of May 8th. The number of people admitted to the centres during the war totalled 36,045, which figure represents those who were actually fed, clothed, and stayed at least one night. It does not include the thousands who used them for a few hours to make enquiries or establish contact with relatives. *They were manned by volunteers, some of whom came from comparatively safe areas to the most vulnerable parts of the City to do the job.*

SHELTERS STAND UP IN A SEA OF DESTRUCTION. MANY LIVES WERE SAVED AS A RESULT OF HULL'S EXTENSIVE CONSTRUCTION OF STREET AND GARDEN SHELTERS.

The aim was to give practical help of a temporary character, advice, sympathy, and the comfort of listening calmly to the tales of distracted mothers or soothe the cries of terrified, and often lost, children, passing them on when the raiding ceased to permanent billets. The aim was achieved in every possible way.

## PERMANENT CENTRES.

The increasing number of damaged houses, the decreasing number of billets available, and the houses unsafe to live in because of the proximity of an unexploded bomb, brought forward the question of providing permanent reception centres. The first four were established in church centres in the most heavily congested areas, and later supplemented by hutments. They were not homes, but enterprise, ingenuity, and the display of understanding by those in control soon produced a homelike and cheerful atmosphere, and contented the displaced until they could make other arrangements with relatives, friends, or neighbours. As opportunity arose they were used for accommodation of overseas marine visitors unable to find beds, or as temporary quarters for essential war workers. In addition, a short-leave hostel for officers of the Women's Forces was set up, as well as a large youth club. These permanent centres, as well as the hostels referred to later, came within the scope of the vast work performed by the Women's Voluntary Services.

## HOSTELS.

For special cases, such as large families, mothers with a number of small children, old people, and cases of special difficulty, hostels were provided, some very large, others of the large family house type of the Victorian period. Two were allocated to the elderly, these alone having been open for more than four years. They were staffed by women of the British Legion.

Other hostels opened were for families, 1,610 people being cared for for different periods. One building was set aside for "other ranks" in the Women's Services on short leave, 9,000 girls being accommodated. For this latter the staffing was done by the Townswomen's Guild on a voluntary basis. In addition, and apart from the Government evacuation schemes, accommodation was provided in the East Riding for 3,000 single men, 2,000 single girls, and over 3,000 people in family hostels. A scheme for transport to and fro was arranged, but happily there was no great call on these centres, which were run by the National Service Hostels Corporation.

## CLOTHING.

A sudden raid, or the deliberate act of people who stayed abed after the Alert had gone, meant that many had to flock to the reception centres in their night attire, and for them clothing had to be provided. Others, who scrambled out with what garments they could muster in the dark, subsequently found that all their possessions had been destroyed by fire. They, too, had to be fitted out to attend the District Offices to make their claims, or to go to work. This clothing was provided through gifts from overseas, the Lord Mayor's Air Raid Distress Fund, or direct purchase.

The volunteers who ran this department had many difficulties to overcome. In the stores there was an unending battle against mice, moths, the climate, etc. These were overcome by weekly airings, the attendance of make-and-mend parties, and the assistance of laundries. Another problem arose over the shortage of goods in the City when the main stores were destroyed, the need of coupons, and the mental

A Communal Shelter

The Wardens on duty in this Post escaped without serious injury.

inability of some people to realise that they were not entitled to a rake-off from anything their eye may rest on. The issue of clothing, the maintenance of stocks, and the making of returns was a sideline compared, for example, with the quelling of fires, but it was a necessary adjunct to the general scheme of things, and was well done.

## THE DISTRESS FUND.

The Lord Mayor's Air Raid Distress Fund was founded in 1940, and was operated in conjunction with the Lord Mayor of London's National Fund. It helped promptly and humanely victims of direct enemy air attacks by supplementing aid from official sources and assisting deserving cases not eligible for grants from Government funds. Altogether £34,000 was disbursed through this medium, and that as quietly and decently as possible. Earlier than this a local Air Raid Distress Fund had been established and did good work, but the Lord Mayor's Fund was the principal means of assistance.

## TRANSPORT.

One section of the Air Raids Welfare Scheme devoted its activities to the provision of transport. At first a voluntary scheme attended to the care of bombed-out people, especially the aged and crippled, who had to be removed from raided areas. The volunteers, most of whom had been at work all day and had their own family problems, faced fire and bombs night after night in this work of mercy. In addition, they salvaged goods from damaged premises, assisted to evacuate hospitals, and transported blood donors to various centres in case of emergency. Later the Corporation Transport Service was used, two buses standing by each night.

## DAMAGED PREMISES.

As showing the difficulties under which the Air Raid Welfare Committee worked, it will perhaps suffice to state that ten reception centres, two hostels, one clothing store, the first central office, and the Welfare Control were destroyed by enemy action. Fifty reception centres, two hostels, and three clothing stores were damaged, but subsequently repaired. Many people, seeing damaged property all around, took these as everyday affairs, little thinking that the work was so essential to the welfare and the morale of the City that the whole organisation had to be pieced together again somehow before darkness fell, to be ready for action again.

## ACKNOWLEDGMENTS.

Few firms or people expect thanks for their contributions to the war effort, but the Air Raid Welfare Committee desire to acknowledge the services of Messrs. T. Hedley & Son, Newcastle, for providing a mobile laundry, and the Associated Soap Manufacturers, Ltd., for a mobile bath, both fully staffed ; the Hull Electricity Department for a mobile electric vacuum cleaner ; a gift of £400 from Hull Master Butchers' Association to provide comforts in the reception centres ; the " Mother Humber " Memorial Fund and Toc H for blankets and clothing in the early difficult days ; and the H.Q. of the Women's Voluntary Service for a 10 h.p. van, a carrier, and a bicycle. The number of religious, charitable and social organisations whose members gave personal assistance is almost beyond count. The war-time trials made all Hull people relatives in spirit if not in blood.

The Meat Market.

The Corporation Transport Garage. Destroyed July, 1941.

## THE DISTRICT OFFICES.

Following the first considerable raid on the City on August 26th, 1940, the Central Welfare office was besieged by people needing advice and services of a dozen different kinds. In consequence, and in collaboration with the Government Assistance Board, it was decided to establish District Offices to be opened in the immediate neighbourhood of a raided area within a matter of hours of the " Raiders Passed " signal. Members of voluntary organisations attended as well as officials of the Corporation Departments, who dealt with such things as billeting orders, travel warrants, removals, cash payments, advice about claims, first aid repairs, emergency ration cards, clothing, filling up of forms, and the like. This meant that the bombed-out had not to travel from one office to another, or even far from their homes, for the District Office came to them.

At one time or another just over 100 such offices were opened in schools, church halls, social halls, and the like, with ample boldly marked notices as to the rooms occupied by different Services. In 331 days 110,850 people were dealt with. This in spite of the fact that the offices were in the main devoid of furniture, generally put into use at a few hours' notice, and to have carried to them, cash, Government documents, writing materials, stationery, typewriters and the like. In very few instances were telephones available. Very often, indeed generally, the administrative staff had themselves spent the night in shelters, or in one form or another of air raid duty.

Since, as already stated, the district offices were in bombed areas, it follows that the buildings were damaged. Rain came in through the roof, snow through broken windows, wind from all quarters. Central heating was rare, food was late, and had to be taken while dealing with a claimant ; comfortable, even reasonable, conditions for work were totally absent. Yet the work went on, often until late in the evening, sometimes till midnight by completely weary people, often with an ear at tension to listen for the new evening " alert " or the boom of the guns.

## BILLETING.

This form of war-time welfare work was once described by a former Minister of Health as " one of the most difficult and thankless tasks laid on Local Authorities." Not unnaturally the dispossessed had a grievance, and since it could not be expended on the members of the Luftwaffe responsible for their unhappiness, some tried to ease themselves by demanding all manner of accommodation from those nearest to hand. It has to be remembered that usually they were very distraught. Some wanted to go in one neighbourhood, some in another. Certain types demanded houses with all manner of modern conveniences. It was the task of the billeting officers to fix them up with shelter immediately, so that the reception centres could be cleared against an influx that same night. This was especially difficult in December-January days, when it was light for a matter of a few hours.

Yet the total number of people billeted was 51,087. The highest on two days was 23,845, following the raids in May, 1941. Other high numbers were 3,580 (February 22nd-25th), 2,754 (March 13th-14th), 3,380 (March 18th), 4,849 (March 31st), and 5,468 (July 18th), all in 1941. It is a tribute to the neighbourly feeling existing in Hull that in no case was it necessary to exercise compulsory billeting powers, though the machinery was at times stretched to the utmost.

Another duty falling to this section of Air Raid Welfare was to find accommodation for thousands of workers drafted into the City to repair damaged property, and for dock workers who arrived from other ports under Ministry orders. Some stayed weeks, others merely days, which added to the complications.

## HOUSES FOR HOMELESS.

In the summer of 1940 the Chief Air Raid Warden, with the help of the men and women in that Service, put into operation a scheme whereby furnished houses could be set at the disposal of families for a few days until they found their own accommodation. Twenty-one empty houses were taken over, and through the generosity of the Wardens, their friends and citizens generally, were equipped with essentials, such as beds, tables, chairs, crockery, cooking utensils, coal, and even a supply of tea and sugar. The Wardens fixed the blackout, and in the course of time found such articles as table cloths, dish cloths, floor cloths, and the like. Moreover, they went over the houses each day to brush round or garnish up as the case may be. Their women companions made it their business to go in to light a fire, have the kettle boiling, and the tea-pot on the table when news came that the house was to be occupied. They were known as the " Good Companions."

The houses were used over and over again, and were of such value that in six months the Ministry of Health gave sanction for it to be officially recognised and for 200 houses to be provided. Once again Hull had set the pace for the Government. Some houses were loaned fully furnished by generous citizens, and the remainder were furnished after a public appeal had been made for household goods.

The people accommodated were families with a number of young children, where the presence of the mother was essential. In other instances families with a bed-ridden member or a child with whooping cough or measles had to be catered for. Expectant mothers were also priority claims for such houses.

After one raid every house was in use. Altogether they were occupied on 662 occasions, by 3,181 people, representing 734 families. The average stay was a matter of a few weeks, though one family was so satisfied and so little concerned with the needs of others that they occupied their house several months.

The late Dr. William Temple, when Archbishop of York, was in Hull in one raid and visited a family so housed. He commented that the scheme was doing more good than anything else to maintain morale. The mother was occupied with her household duties, the father could go to work knowing that all was well, and in the evening the family could consult together as to the next and best step to take.

## REHOUSING AND REMOVALS.

The City Treasurer's Department took over the task of being responsible for arranging accommodation in houses, hostels, etc., and for removals in appropriate cases. For this purpose two representatives attended District Offices for the whole of the time these were open. The number of removals arranged was 7,939, of which 1,086 were out-of-town. Over 2,350 homeless families were put in Corporation houses, in private houses requisitioned for the purpose, or into other private houses for which tenancies could be arranged. More than 1,600 people were accommodated in hostels for various periods, and 734 families (3,181 persons) fixed up in furnished houses. The maximum number of the latter held at one time was 152.

In addition all Government stores of furniture, clothing and general equipment, as well as those purchased locally, came within the purview of the City Treasurer's Department. They covered 183 distinct kinds, and totalled 242,682 single articles. A financial statement shows that in 1941-42 £40,285 was spent in shelter and feeding stations alone. There were Government grants, of course, but from September, 1939, to March, 1944, this one branch of Air Raid Welfare cost the ratepayers a matter of over £13,000.

## STORAGE AND SALVAGE.

No one likes to lose anything. A woman certainly hates to lose her home, for it is the centre of her life. Hence, though the salvage and storage of furniture was an unspectacular part of Air Raid Welfare work, it was a mighty important one. Without this branch household goods would have been left in the ruins of a house, or at best in a building minus windows, perhaps even a roof, at the mercy of rain, snow, or fog, and also at the disposal of evil people who wandered round after a raid seeking what they could find. Hence the business of salvage, removal and storage of furniture came under the direction of the City Engineer. The men of his Department, in conjunction with local removal contractors and at times assisted by West Riding firms, removed or stored 2,809 homes. One way or another, they made 12,438 removals, for the furniture of some families was handled four and even five times—from bombed site to storage, from storage to the new house, to require removal again in another raid, and, finally, perhaps be taken to a country area or distant town.

In one night in March, 1941, 400 houses were rendered uninhabitable. In the May raids of that year the demand for space was such that all the accommodation available was taken and requisitioning was resorted to. The Corporation Fruit Market had to be used, and more than that, a stretch of land in the East Park turned into a site for a temporary storehouse " built " of wood and tarpaulins, the latter specially released by the Ministry of Works.

It was not, of course, a matter merely of removing articles. Complete records had to be maintained, inventories prepared for the satisfaction of the owner and for official records. Unhappily the contents of several hundred homes were eventually lost through damage or destruction of some of the places used as warehouses in subsequent raids, but much fine work was done, and that at a time when the wife and mother, to whom the home meant so much, was distracted with grief or shock, or both, and unable to attend with any degree of efficiency to anything.

In the early days the Government allowance for removals was limited to £5, later increased to £10. The bombed-out had to pay anything above this, and at times resort was made to the Lord Mayor's Air Raid Distress Fund. At such a time, however, it was not money that mattered so much as service, and that is where this Department stepped in.

## INFORMATION.

To save people running round in circles asking news of relatives who may have been killed or injured in a raid an Information Bureau was set up. Though helped considerably by members of the W.V.S. and other voluntary workers, the changes, owing to calling-up or other causes, in the end meant that the staff of the

A Social Centre is hit. The Young People's Institute in George Street.

School building damaged in Londesborough Street.

City Libraries had to bear almost the whole burden. Sometimes the demands were such that the Libraries had to be closed for certain hours. Indeed, at one period the Central Library had to be closed for eleven days and the Branch Libraries for fifteen days so that the staff could concentrate on this particular work.

The scheme followed was to send a representative to all District Offices to obtain news of casualties and keep contact with Wardens, Police, etc., and docket the information so gathered. Hence a caller at the Central Library was able to learn the whereabouts of the body of a relative who had been killed, the hospital caring for someone wounded, the new address of a bombed-out family, the town or village to which people had been evacuated. Later on it became possible to tell citizens the new address of a bombed-out business firm, the Post Office the whereabouts of a family compelled to move. In short, the staff of the Information Bureau went round in intelligent circles to save countless others running round with no sense of direction, wasting their own time and that of officials at a period when time was valuable and nerves a little strained.

Altogether, information was obtained about 127,350 individuals, 47,842 families, and 1,257 business firms. It was handed on to 18,465 known inquirers at the central office alone; the inquiries at branch offices were at times so heavy that it was impossible to spare the time to make a note of the inquirer or inquiry. What was known was told, and the next inquirer turned to.

In addition to these personal calls, letters and telegrams came from many parts of Great Britain and overseas, these sometimes necessitating a searcher service, that is, the staff pursued inquiries which normally would have been done by a relative. The same process was followed to find information for Government and local organisations.

Another phase of the work of this section was the manning of loud speaker vans to tell people in bombed areas where to go and what to do, and of contacting the local Rediffusion Service to get last minute news into the homes of the people. This was a very valuable help in the maintenance of good morale.

In between these duties the Libraries staff managed to collect and give to the various Civil Defence and Welfare Services, hospitals, etc., no fewer than 28,000 books.

EMERGENCY FEEDING.

When the war broke out the Hull Corporation had only one kitchen, with a capacity for something like 2,000 meals. It was used for school children's meals. Before the heavy raiding began the Town Clerk reported that a scheme was in operation under which 47,000 two-course meals could be served every three hours. It had been planned to erect new kitchens, but building restrictions killed this, so arrangements were made with local catering and manufacturing firms to place all their resources at the disposal of the Corporation in case of emergency. Cafes and out-sales departments were established, mobile kitchens obtained, and transport scheduled to carry food from one section of the City to another. Moreover, the scheme was so built up as to provide that in the event of the east part of the City being divided from the west through the combination of raids and the presence of the River Hull, no serious hitch would occur. The two divisions could work as a whole or separately.

Stocks of food, including thousands of large tins of meat and stew, were secured

A DIRECT HIT ON ASKEW AVENUE SCHOOL.

FOREST OF DESTRUCTION. GAUNT REMAINS OF HULL INDUSTRIAL PREMISES.

and stored, and since crockery was unobtainable, 100,000 wax containers and spoons were purchased. All this was done before the Ministry of Food stepped in with a circular offering advice and indicating that it was prepared to make available to Local Authorities supplies of food and equipment. This was in March, 1941. The food arrived on the afternoon of May 7th, was sorted and packed ready for distribution, and destroyed that same night in the big raid.

Indeed, that same night the Emergency Feeding Scheme as a whole came in for severe losses in personnel, food, mobile canteens, cafes, and, worst of all, the main kitchen. Yet it was functioning by 1 a.m., serving breakfasts at 5-30, and one way or another prepared and served 27,000 meals during the day. This was achieved partly through the premises which had escaped damage, the mobile canteens available, the introduction of twenty more from the West Riding, and the temporary establishment of new centres.

The serving had scarcely ceased, certainly order had not been restored, when the " Alert " sounded again. In that raid centres with seating capacity for 6,000 people were destroyed, but despite the exhaustion of the staff from the two raids and the tiring work, 40,000 meals were served to the homeless, the various Defence Services (Firemen, Wardens, Rescue Squads, etc.) and those who could not get home to a meal owing to the dislocation of transport. In seventeen days in May (8th to 24th) 500,000 meals were served, besides tea, cakes and sandwiches being always available, by a service nigh to paralysed on the night of the 7th of the month.

That speaks for the efficiency of the scheme as designed and built up, and the loyalty and endurance of the staff and voluntary helpers.

In July, during which there were four major raids apart from the tip and run variety, 120,000 meals were prepared and served. Nor were they cold collations.

In mid-summer of 1941, despite the losses in the May raids, the Department had running nine town cafes, four dock cafes, twenty-one out-sales centres and four kitchens, besides thirty mobile canteens. The crews of these, generally women, found their way to raided areas despite obstructions, gaping shell holes in the roads, and entanglements of telephone and trolley wires.

SICK BAYS.

The Medical Officer's Department undertook the responsibility of establishing and running two sick bays, places apart from either hospitals or first aid posts.

Their purpose was to supply accommodation for people suffering slight injury or shock, needing treatment for a few days or a few weeks. Invalids or convalescents were taken there when their homes were hit ; so were homeless persons taken ill while living in billets or centres, and hospital and nursing home cases evacuated suddenly on account of structural damage or anxiety over an unexploded bomb. Late in the war, when lull periods were somewhat lengthy, chronic, sick or infirm cases were taken from homes which had suffered air raid damage, but the number was limited owing to the need to maintain empty beds for raid nights. In addition, eight subsidiary sick bays, with beds ranging from two to eight, were available to deal with cases of sickness occurring at reception centres.

Altogether, just over 100 beds were available, and though there was a minimum number of paid nurses, much valuable work was done by members of the V.A.D., British Red Cross Society and Order of St. John.

MESSRS. STEWART & CRAIG'S PREMISES, HEDON ROAD.

## MEDICAL REST CENTRES.

Another responsibility of the M.O's Department was the running of a medical rest centre to deal with contagious cases such as scabies, measles and impetigo from reception centres. Though the number of patients totalled only thirty-four, their separation from other people driven to communal centres for shelter went a long way towards preventing any epidemic of skin diseases or worse.

## POST-RAID WORK.

Before closing this section dealing with the Air Raid Welfare Organisation, it is fitting that reference should be made to the City Architect's Department and the Committee responsible for co-operation with the Food Office. Members of the Architect's staff commenced work a few hours after a raid. They had to classify the damage done to buildings, decide if it was reasonably safe for a family to occupy a building, report on repairs, and generally notify all Departments concerned with the rehousing of the bombed out, the storage of their furniture, and the payment of billeting allowances, of the conditions existing.

The work of those co-operating with the Food Office was to see that Emergency Ration Cards were issued to bombed out, and to arrange for fresh supplies for areas in which shops had been destroyed. The result was that there was always sufficient food available. At no time was there a shortage of food in the City, or a breakdown in transport. Altogether 60,500 emergency cards were distributed.

# THE VITAL LINK

### POST OFFICE NEVER BROKE DOWN

It is well known that many members of the Post Office staffs up and down the country are ex-sailors or ex-soldiers, liable to be called up in the event of national emergency; that other specialists such as telegraph men must form the nucleus of the signal sections of the Forces; that sorters and the like are at once asked for when war breaks out in order that those in uniform may keep a link with home.

Thus, in the matter of loss of Post Office staff, Hull suffered to the same extent as other centres of like importance, but the comparison ends there, for not only was the Head Post Office the target for a direct hit, and sub-post offices sufferers to a lesser extent, but there was a heavy increase of work following every raid caused by anxious people all over the country telegraphing their relatives.

Despite all the handicaps and all the strain, only once did the service falter; that was when there was a delay of half an hour in starting the morning delivery after a heavy raid.

When a letter could not be delivered owing to the destruction of a house it was not " Returned to sender " It was held until it was known to which reception centre the addressee had been sent, or retained until the police or Information Bureau could provide reliable information regarding the address. In the course of the war there were 3,000 instances of such extra and voluntary service.

So much for sorting and delivery.

The Factory of Messrs. J. H. Fenner, Ltd., Marfleet.

## BLOWN FROM THEIR SWITCHBOARDS.

The counter work was equally increased, despite depletion in staffs, for there were parcels for the troops to handle and generally register; payments had to be made to dependents; and, in countless cases, new forms and books to be issued to people who had lost such articles in the course of a raid.

As to the telephone department, there was an occasion when the girls were literally blown from their switchboards by the force of an explosion, in spite of which they maintained the service, so vital to military and civil defence needs. Hull's telephones, once the first fear of giving information to an enemy plane had passed, were never silent except for an actual breakdown in the line. And that brings us to the Engineers' Section.

In addition to routine duties, these men were called out on 50 occasions to deal with bomb damage to vital lines of communication. Once there was the complete destruction of part of an underground track and cables containing up to 2,000 individual wires. At another time a 21-way underground track containing, among others, six main trunk cables was demolished, while in the same raid another track containing three main cables was badly damaged in three places. Water and debris impeded the work, and sometimes craters had to be bridged by cables slung from telegraph poles and lamp standards. In that one raid over 8,000 wires had to be jointed to effect temporary repairs alone. Yet the work went on, day and night, in snow and rain, so that people could communicate one with the other locally or maintain contact with the country generally. Only the technicians will know the skill, ingenuity and makeshift methods which had to be employed, but Hull people generally realised and appreciated the work of the Hull G.P.O. staff during the war.

In addition, the Hull G.P.O. maintained its own Home Guard unit, 300 strong, with 19 women auxiliaries. Their services in their own special capacity were of the greatest value to the military authorities.

# THE FIRE GUARD

Though not called upon actively to function as a separate organisation, the Fire Guard Service was set up, by Government decree, towards the end of 1943. Prior to this the responsibility for the organisation of the perhaps more generally known " fire-watchers " was undertaken by the Warden Service.

Considerable work was put in on the development and organisation of the Government's new " Fire Guard Plan," and by June of 1944 the new Service had carried out its first efficiency tests and was ready for full operation.

Many hundreds of people were trained and undertook duties in connection with the Business Premises schemes and in street parties—many of whom, in addition, carried out duties in one or other of the Civil Defence Services.

There is little doubt that had the necessity arisen this Service would have proved to be a vital part of the defence against incendiary attacks and, by " on the spot " action, have prevented much serious fire damage.

## IN CASE OF INVASION

Had the Germans landed in the East Riding and attempted to take control of Hull they would have found that quite a lot had been done to impede and handicap them. Members of the staff of all sections of the City Engineer's Department, in full accord with those in authority at Garrison Command, were involved, and were supplied with secret instructions regarding the work to be done.

For example, the bridges over the River Hull were to be immobilised, not by being blown up, but by having vital mechanical parts removed. Thus bacule bridges would face the roads like a wall, permitting vessels to be navigated, but blocking all foot and mechanical transport. Swing bridges would be so fixed as to make the turntable inoperative. The parts were to be taken out of the city, but, if this were impossible, plans were made whereby the machinery would have been buried in a pit in the City. The driver was not to know his destination until the crisis arose, when he would have been given sealed orders.

The Victoria Pier would have been left alone, but it was arranged that the approach bridge to the pontoon should be picked up on the supports at the south end and the pontoon sunk in position. All vessels lying in the Old Harbour were to be cleared under the authority of a naval officer, a body of watermen having an intimate knowledge of the area volunteering to work under him.

Petrol supplies were to be dealt with on receipt of instructions of the Garrison Commander.

Chanterlands Avenue subway would have been flooded from Setting Dyke, this job being left to the fire brigade to deal with.

All transport vehicles, except those essential for the vital final hours, would have been immobilised, as would also all mobile compressors, generators and other highway plant, by the removal of vital parts. Oxygen, acetylene, fuel oil, etc., would have been destroyed.

Plans of a similar technical character were made by the Corporation Electricity Department concerning the power station.

Happily, the need for these drastic measures did not arise, but the plans made received the approval and commendation of the Garrison Commander.

The facts are recorded here as showing part of the unseen work done by the staffs of the Corporation and the various sections of the Civil Defence Service.

## THE PRESS

HULL *DAILY MAIL* AND *TIMES*.

It is not without a degree of pride that the Hull *Daily Mail* and *Times* can claim that throughout the five years of war in a City which received a heavy share of the enemy's hatred, the full publication of all their issues was maintained.

Despite severely restricted paper supplies, the destruction of cargoes of paper at sea or in depots ashore ; despite considerable damage done to the head office by heavy bomb blast, and at times complete or partial telephonic, telegraphic, private wire and rail isolation, all the urgent calls of the public for the latest war news were met.

The Hull *Daily Mail* was very fortunate during those terrible nights of vicious bombing of the city by the Luftwaffe. All around the building large shops, offices, a builders' exchange, public houses, many dwelling houses, etc., were demolished by bomb and fire. Employees of the firm coming to work in the morning following the many raids were obliged to scramble through debris, past burning buildings, over many lines of hose. And yet the *Mail* buildings in Jameson Street continued to stand like an island in a sea of desolation and destruction.

On the night of March 21st, 1941, a very heavy calibre high explosive bomb fell at the rear of the *Mail* buildings. It demolished the popular Metropole Dance Hall, the Builders' Exchange, a number of shops and two public houses. West Street had suffered badly by the explosion of this bomb. The *Mail* office also suffered considerably.

## THE YORKSHIRE POST.

The Branch Office of *The Yorkshire Post* and *The Yorkshire Evening Post*, Paragon House, Paragon Street, was destroyed by the fire which swept the centre of the City during the vicious air attack on the night of May 7th-8th, 1941. The office formed part of a newly-built block of property, the whole of which was demolished. Spreading rapidly from adjacent buildings, notably a furniture store in Chariot Street and the Neptune Hotel in Paragon Street, the fire enveloped the office so quickly as to endanger the lives of the caretaker and his family, for whom emergency accommodation had been provided in the basement, otherwise they might have been trapped in their permanent quarters at the top of the building.

Despite the total destruction of the office, emergency arrangements ensured contact with the Head Offices in Leeds and a report of the raid, as full as security reasons would allow, was being printed in *The Yorkshire Post* and *The Yorkshire Evening Post* while portions of the Branch Office were still burning. Because of the temporary dislocation of the trunk telephone service one of the reporters travelled to York by car and telephoned the report from the Branch Office there to Leeds.

Typical of the general desire to find accommodation for bombed-out staffs were the generous offers received. The writing room and telephones at the Royal Station Hotel were at the staff's disposal; there was an offer of accommodation at the Corporation's Electricity Showrooms, and, later, while arrangements were being made for the occupation of temporary premises in Albion Street, the staff had the use of editorial offices of the Hull *Daily Mail*.

The Albion Street office, already bomb-battered, narrowly escaped the fate of Paragon House in the raid of June 23rd-24th, 1943, when the near-by Municipal Museum, then in temporary occupation by Thornton-Varley, Ltd., was totally destroyed.

## CONTROLLER SAYS "THANK YOU"
### MEN AND WOMEN WHO UNDERTOOK ARDUOUS DUTIES

The publication of this book has a two-fold purpose. One is the provision of some historical record of the hostile air attacks on the City during the World War 1939-1945, and so refute many incorrect rumours and reports; the other is to express appreciation of the outstanding services rendered by officials and citizens.

The book is a recapitulation of combined operations of Civil Defence Services, and contains little about the individuals in charge. My responsibilities were limited to the A.R.P. Services, which included the Warden, Rescue, Control and Report Centre, Cyclist Messenger, Motor Cyclist Messenger, Casualty, Gas Identification, and Decontamination Services, but there were many other sections which, though directly responsible to their own Ministries, had to collaborate most intimately with the Civil Defence team. These included the Police, National Fire Service (originally A.F.S.), Public Utility Services, namely Electricity, Water, British Gas, East Hull Gas, Hessle Gas, Telephone, Transport, Railways, Post Office, Broadcast Relay, and the British Broadcasting Corporation together with many ancillary services, for example, Food Office, Evacuation Section of the Education Department, City Architect's Department, Parks Department (for weather forecast), W.V.S., Information Bureau, Dogs' Home and R.S.P.C.A., Animal Guards, all religious denominations, Chamber of Commerce, Chamber of Trade, Port Authority, and the larger industrial concerns. Very close contact was necessary in the preparatory stages, and when action commenced the liaison work with the Admiralty, Military, Air Force, Regional Commissioner's Office and the Ministry of Home Security proved its value.

The Active Forces had many plans for the reception or diversion of the enemy which had to operate within seconds, as an example in the event of sea or air-borne invasion, and the team-work between the Communications Section of Civil Defence and these Active Forces was excellent. Few of the public are aware that it was part of the functions of the Control and Report Centre Service to ensure rapid signals indicating the necessity of setting up diversionary plans, and I wish to express my appreciation and the thanks of this City to the staff for their untiring efforts.

To me has been given the privilege of conveying a word of thanks to all those responsible for the planning and execution of operation, and the preparation of reports which form the basis of this publication, since they cannot include remarks which are appropriate to their own efforts.

It will be better to deal with these Services in order of sequence of events and commence with the Wardens, as it was their primary responsibility to report dropping of enemy missiles. Mr. R. G. Tarran was appointed Chief Warden before the outbreak of hostilities, putting much energy into the preparatory plan, and when raiding commenced, was equally energetic to improve and amend the organisation to suit changing circumstances.

The wardens' messages were conveyed by the Communications Branch, comprising cyclist messengers, motor cyclists, and the Control and Report Centres. The Cyclist Messenger Service was under the able control of the Honorary Commandant, Alderman Frederick Holmes, who took over when each Service had a few messengers as a part of their own section. These he welded into a common pool, and although his health undoubtedly suffered as a result of the work he put into the organisation, one always had confidence and felt that his department could be relied upon; indeed, he was never known to fail to supply messengers for A.R.P., N.F.S., or the W.V.S. The motor cyclist messengers were primarily for long-distance journeys, such as York and Leeds, but on many occasions they undertook the longer journeys within the City, and to those to whom the responsibility of leadership fell—for as they were called up, frequent changes had to be made—I cannot be too grateful. Communications were dominated by the Control and Report Centres, and to Messrs. Torr, Graby, Whitehead and Owen, the Superintendents, and Mr. Duncan, the Liaison Officer, I record this appreciation of their loyal and devoted service.

The priority Service was always Rescue, and in Mr. Wm. Morris, a Corporation official of skill and ability, we had a man whose planning in his capacity as the City Engineer made it obvious that he would make a first-class job of such an important Service. He placed his department at our disposal for the scheme for the rescue of trapped persons and for the gigantic works programme. The award of the honour of the O.B.E. was a fitting tribute to the services he rendered, for spectacular as the operational work of rescue may be, it cannot be efficient unless the person in charge of the administration is aware of the needs of the party on the site, and can efficiently organise so that there will be no shortage or delay of men or equipment.

The Casualty Service gives immediate aid to the injured and removes them to skilled assistance. To the Medical Officer of Health, Dr. N. Gebbie, was allotted the task of organising the Service and co-ordinating the hospital arrangements. This Service carried out their duties in a most efficient manner, and on numerous occasions casualties, after having received treatment, expressed their appreciation.

When we were so unfortunate as to lose the services of Dr. Diamond, the Deputy Medical Officer of Health, who was killed at his post of duty, the Emergency Committee, on the recommendation of Dr. Gebbie, appointed Dr. J. N. Wheatley as C.D. Medical Officer. Coming to the City when heavy raids were commencing, his experience in the London blitz and medical knowledge proved of great assistance.

It would be incomplete if the Mortuary Service were not mentioned, for they undertook a most difficult task with efficiency and promptitude.

The Police, whose normal duties particularly fitted them to deal with air raid incidents, were made responsible for the Incident Officer Service, and provided bomb reconnaissance officers, the latter augmented by the Warden Service. The police officer, regular, reserve, or special, was also charged with the duty of reporting as if he were a warden, and on many occasions information came from that source. Their co-operation with the Warden Service was exemplary, and there have been cases of healthy competition to see how many incendiary bombs either side could extinguish in excess of the other. As the war progressed, there was a collective increase in duties imposed upon the Police Service, including search for anti-personnel bombs, evacuation for UXB's, etc., and I desire to thank most sincerely both Mr. T. Howden, who was Chief Constable when the war commenced, and Mr. Thomas Wells, who succeeded him in 1941, for their co-operation, which was at all times so much in evidence.

The National Fire Service, originally the A.F.S., was in the early days under the control of the Chief Constable, and though a separate organisation, never failed to give the utmost co-operation at all levels with Civil Defence. Mr. T. H. Barker, the first Fire Force Commander, was later succeeded by Mr. J. H. Pilling, and I am deeply grateful to them and their personnel for all that was done to assist Civil Defence.

The Utility Services are many, but each, in its respective sphere, is absolutely essential to the life of the community. The Corporation were fortunate in having such an excellent organisation as existed in the Electricity Department, and the provision of an A.R.P. scheme was efficiently dealt with by the General Manager, Mr. D. Bellamy. Before hostilities commenced, his senior engineer attended the Home Office school and obtained the highest training degree issued. Had it not been for this anticipation of the department's needs, it may be that the supply might not have been maintained with the efficiency that was noticeable during enemy activity. The installations suffered considerable damage, and it took all the ingenuity, perspicacity and determination of the General Manager and his staff to overcome the difficulties. The public have little idea of the work behind the scenes and the problems and dangers that had to be faced to preserve the continuity of supply. With the exception of the immediate locality of the points of impact, there was so little interruption that the service was taken for granted and it is very necessary that this tribute should be paid to the department. The award of the honour of the O.B.E. made to Lieut.-Colonel Bellamy for activities in the Anti-Aircraft Regiment should be regarded equally as an appreciation of his exemplary management of the Electricity Department.

The distress of the public if ever the water supply had failed needs no comment, but the excellent management of the Water Department by Mr. T. H. Jones and his deputy, Mr. C. Green, prevented such a misfortune befalling the City. In spite of tremendous odds, and on one occasion knowing the slender threads upon which his equipment relied, and being aware that a large scale raid was imminent, he encouraged his Service and organised his staff ready for improvisation should it have been necessary. On a few occasions the public had to suffer a little inconvenience, and stand pipes had to be used, but this and the rapid restoration is evidence of the fact that the Water Engineer and Manager was determined that his Service should not fail.

The Gas Companies had an excellent mutual arrangement, and although the greater amount of work fell upon Messrs. Higham and Hammerton, the Managers of the British and East Hull Gas Companies respectively, they had an excellent Liaison Officer in Mr. J. Byrne. Incidentally, he attended at the Control Centre on every night throughout the war, and his knowledge of the Service was most useful when decisions had to be taken quickly. The Gas Companies were not quite so fortunate in the maintenance of supply, as restoration is difficult when mains are flooded, but the problems were tackled with resource and ingenuity, with the result that there was never more than a few days before pressure was available.

The Transport Department has had two Managers, Mr. J. Lawson and Mr. G. H. Pulfrey, and it was during Mr. Pulfrey's time that the heaviest raiding occurred, and his organisation faced several major disasters. The central garage and many buses were destroyed at the same time as the administrative offices, and the sub-depots were considerably damaged, but the Service never failed. The public have every reason to be grateful to the Transport Department for their excellent effort in restoring normal services with such speed.

Mr. T. Holme, the Telephone Manager, was never in any doubt as to the importance of his Service, and organised excellent alternative means of communication. When cables or premises were wrecked he had available a scheme which could reasonably quickly be put into operation. No previous planning, however, could overcome the broken cable, and the repair of such an incident meant nothing but laborious toil. His staff, however, worked excellently and dealt with the problem of the destruction of the Central Exchange and the selection of priority lines for restoration, extremely well. When Mr. Holme retired, towards the end of the war, it was freely admitted that his had been a marvellously efficient Service, and one deserving real praise.

The L.N.E.R. suffered much material damage, but it was the Fire Services which were most in demand at their incidents. When, however, any co-operation was required, it was always readily available, and to Mr. L. Ballan, O.B.E., who was the District Superintendent during the raids, must go the thanks of this City for an organisation which stood up to its tests extremely well.

The Director of Education, Mr. R. C. Moore, undertook the responsibility for evacuation of children and the aged and infirm, and a very elaborate scheme was prepared before the outbreak of hostilities. After the initial arrangements had been carried out, there were always numbers to be evacuated at fairly regular intervals, and the scheme worked very well indeed.

The classification of and dealing with air raid damage, including emergency repairs, was very ably managed by Mr. A. Rankine ; he, together with his staff, gave splendid assistance to achieve the almost impossible.

The dissemination of information following a raid was organised by Mr. J. Cranshaw, the Chief Librarian, and on the many occasions the plan was used it fulfilled a very necessary service in the part of public life, for without this the citizens would often have been at a loss to know where food, water, and other necessities were available.

The Parks Superintendent gave us admirable assistance with weather reports, and enabled us on many occasions to anticipate enemy moves.

There are many other public services which must be mentioned : the Broadcast Relay Service, managed by Mr. H. F. G. Evered ; the various organisations for the care of animals ; the Municipal Restaurants and emergency feeding schemes ; road repair and departments responsible for the clearance of roads and highways. To the Hull Chemists' Associations for their assistance with the Bleach Cream Scheme, and to all of those Services, their managers and staffs, sincere thanks are extended for their co-operation.

The welfare of the citizens was under the jurisdiction of the Air Raid Welfare Committee, comprising Councillor G. Russell (Chairman), Councillor J. D. L. Nicholson (Lord Mayor) (Deputy Chairman), Alderman Mrs. Slimming and Alderman Coult. This committee was ably assisted by the Town Clerk, in whom the City was fortunate in having an official who not only co-operated with the Civil Defence in all its major problems, but also one who spared no personal effort to assist in every possible manner, and who was, in turn, so far as Welfare matters were concerned, most efficiently assisted by Mr. H. G. Freeman, the Director of Social Welfare. This committee had the very able assistance of the W.V.S., under their joint organisers, Mrs. Morton Stewart, M.B.E., and Miss D. Robinson, O.B.E. How much this City owes to these two ladies and their staff will never be known. Apart from the onerous responsibilities connected with the homeless, billeting, rehousing, feeding, reception centres, distribution of clothing, and other kinds of assistance, they had many other tasks not directly concerned with enemy activity, but they faced all these duties with equal cheerfulness, and it was always a pleasure to ask for assistance from them, knowing it would be forthcoming.

The supply of equipment to a Civil Defence organisation where there were some 120,000 personnel was an enormous task, but it did not deter the City Treasurer, Mr. C. H. Pollard, O.B.E., and the staff of his Central Stores Department. At all times they maintained the flow of equipment to fit personnel, furnish a Service, or replace any that may have been lost. The scheme of distribution was excellent and the equally difficult task of disposal of surplus was handled with the same efficiency as was in evidence during the building-up process.

The Gas Identification Service was controlled by Mr. D. J. T. Bagnall, the City Analyst, and whilst the Service did not function in its original capacity, it was on many occasions of the greatest assistance to other Services, as, for example, the recognition of the original and confirmation of subsequent phosphorus bombs. The City Analyst was a most appropriate choice for this Service.

The Decontamination Service, fortunately, was not called upon to operate, but nevertheless Mr. J. Ward, the Public Cleansing Superintendent, had a difficult task in organising and bringing the Service to a state of efficiency, for it was generally admitted that this was an unpleasant job, and it took most of his persistence to persuade the personnel of the importance of their duties, especially during long periods of inactivity. There is no doubt that the Service was always ready for duty if it ever had been required, and combined with the arrangements made by Mr. G. Tootell, the Baths Superintendent, for the treatment of contaminated clothing, the City had a scheme which would have dealt with a poison-gas attack equally as efficiently as the other Services dealt with fire and high explosives.

Towards the end of the war the Government decided that a separate Fire Guard organisation should be set up, and where it was already part of the Warden Service, it should be divorced therefrom and a Fire Guard Officer appointed. Hull was well served by Major T. D. G. Napier, who came from London. In the face of considerable difficulties he built up a Service ready for operations, but although there were one or two minor raids after he took up office, there was never anything sufficiently serious to extend the Service.

There remain to be mentioned the Services connected with the Active Forces and the various Departments of the Region. These officials were at all times most helpful, and the Regional Commissioner, General Sir William Bartholomew, G.C.B., and the officers on his staff, always arrived most promptly and brought to bear the resources under their jurisdiction which were available for the alleviation of the City's difficulties.

My colleagues on the Emergency Committee, by name, Aldermen Schultz, Stark and Holmes, and Councillors Chapman, Honor and Russell, were, from the commencement, fully aware of the responsibility placed upon themselves as members of the Committee and as Deputy Controllers, and also placed upon myself in the joint capacity of their Chairman and Controller. This Committee, as a whole, were amongst the first in the City to join the Civil Defence Service as volunteers, and continued in that capacity.

Each member was responsible for a branch of the Service, with the added responsibility of Deputy Chairman to Alderman Schultz. It was unfortunate that regulations did not permit them to be appointed as Deputy Controllers of the respective sections, but they were, however, allocated to the various divisions of the City and took up their action posts on each attack. Whilst communications were maintained they kept me informed of the position in the area, and on the few occasions when the area became isolated, they took command of the local situation. When the general incidence of attack was known they toured the areas affected and passed forward Situation Reports, which made possible a general appreciation of the effect on the City. The very condensed reports which appeared in the press and elsewhere following the raids gave little indication of the team-work which made up the channel of communications preceding the announcements, and the practical experience and knowledge which each member gathered in his duties as Deputy Controller (more often than not whilst the raid was in progress) was invaluable when it came to the innumerable committee meetings and post-raid conferences, where schemes were formulated to overcome the effect of the raid. As each problem came up for discussion, at least one or two of the members would have personal knowledge of the situation under review, thus materially assisting deliberations. Hence it was with considerable regret that the Committee acceded to the Government's instruction that dual appointments should be discontinued, and I was succeeded as Chairman by Councillor Russell, and the Deputy Chairmanship passed to Alderman Stark, and the remainder of the Committee relinquished their appointments as Deputy Controllers. The old principles, however, continued, and although there was the formal change of official appointment, the team continued as before with Alderman Schultz as Deputy Controller. I cannot be too grateful to my colleagues for their determination to do their utmost to carry out their duties with the maximum of benefit and efficiency. From the Committee point of view, they abandoned all political aspects of the normal Council procedure, and I can very truthfully say that every Committee decision was considered only from the aspect of which was the better for the City, and I certainly cannot remember anything other than a unanimous resolution. From the operational standpoint, they had similar views as Deputy Controllers, and I do most earnestly ask the public to keep in mind the one outstanding factor which is, more often than not, disregarded : that the enemy had, as its main objective, the destruction of life, property and communications, and to cause as much confusion as possible. It follows, therefore, that every raid must bring confusion of some sort, and the problem of the Committee was not, as is so often imagined, to prevent this confusion, but rather to resolve it as rapidly as possible, and judging from the efforts made and the results obtained, there is not the slightest doubt that they did an excellent job, and I am proud to have been associated with them in their task.

In conclusion, I wish personally to thank the Regional Commissioners ; the Lord Mayors and Sheriffs who held office from the outbreak of war ; Members of the Kingston upon Hull City Council, Heads of the Civil Defence Services, and all the chief officials of the Authority who were connected with Civil Defence, either directly or indirectly ; the Heads of the Utility Services ; the District Superintendent of the Railway Company ; the Garrison Commanders who held office ; the officers in charge of the Naval Base, the Anti-Aircraft Regiments, the Royal Air Force, and the Observer Corps ; the thousands of volunteers who did duty at Control and Report Centres and in one or other of the Civil Defence Services ; the full-time members of those Services, the Regional Staff ; the general public for their assistance and patience ; and, particularly, the Emergency Committee as a whole, the A.R.P. Officer, Mr. E. Edwards, M.B.E., to whom much praise must go for his technical knowledge, ability and loyalty ; Mr. J. B. Tomlinson, the Committee Clerk, and the many individuals who gave me personally such loyal service.

*Leonard Spearghs.*

CONTROLLER.

# CITY AND COUNTY OF KINGSTON UPON HULL
## SCHEDULE OF RAIDS IN WHICH BOMBS WERE DROPPED

R - Railway
D - Domestic
I - Industrial

| Date | Red Hrs. | White Hrs. | Area affected | Time of first bomb | Incendiaries (Clusters) | Ks. 50 cwt. 1 | Ks. 250 cwt. 5 | Ks. 500 cwt. 10 | Ks. 1000 cwt. 20 | Ks. 1800 cwt. 36 | Mines P.M. Ks. 1000 cwt. 20 | Mines G.M. Ks. 1000 cwt. 20 | Weight per raid in cwt. | Remarks | Damage | Casualties K. | Casualties S.I. |
|---|---|---|---|---|---|---|---|---|---|---|---|---|---|---|---|---|---|
| 20-6-40 | 01.00 | 04.02 | Chapman Street Railway Bridge | | 1 | 1 | | | | | | | 1 | Bridge parapet slightly damaged | R. | Nil | |
| 26-6-40 | 00.10 | 03.19 | Chamberlain Road to Lodge Street | 01.40 | | 11 | | | | | | | 11 | Domestic property slight damage | D. | | 1 |
| 30-7-40 | 00.05 | 00.53 | Porter Street and Great Passage Street | 00.10 | | 2 | | | | | | | 2 | Flats in Great Passage Street and Porter Street damaged | D. | | |
| 25-8-40 | 02.31 | 01.57 | Carlton, Eastbourne, and Rustenburg and Morrill Streets | 02.31 | | | 8 | | | | | | 40 | Anderson damaged at Rustenburg Street. Domestic damage | D. | 6 | 10 |
| 25/26-8-40 | 20.59 | 00.20 | Alexandra and Victoria Docks | 21.44 | 3 | | | | | | | | | Incendiaries quickly put out | | | |
| 27/28-8-40 | 20.46 | 03.29 | Maternity Home, Hedon Road, Seward Street | 02.31 | | 3 | | | | | | | 3 | Lodge and Maternity Home destroyed. Seward Street Goods Station damaged | R.D. | | |
| 30-8-40 | 01.50 | 03.01 | Bellamy Street, Williamson Street and Victoria Dock | 02.20 | | 9 | 1 | | | | | | 14 | First H.E. to straddle docks. Slight damage | R.D. | | 1 |
| 3-9-40 | 00.09 | 01.50 | In River east of King George Dock (?) | 01.19 | | | | | | | | | | Unknown number H.E. in River | | | 1 |
| 4/5-9-40 | 20.55 | 00.25 | Incendiary raid only. Dalton and Tower Streets | 21.15 | 2 | | | | | | | | | Incendiaries quickly extinguished | | | |
| 6-9-40 | 05.10 | 05.55 | Incendiary raid only. James Reckitt Avenue, Chamberlain Road | 05.20 | 4 | | | | | | | | | Mostly fell in fields, no fires started | | | |
| 10-9-40 | 22.06 | 22.58 | Incendiary raid only. Telford, Steynburg, Margaret Streets | 23.30 | 2 | | | | | | | | | Few fires started, quickly put out | | | |
| 24-9-40 | 03.51 | 05.43 | Incendiary raid only. Maybury Road and Belfield Avenue | 04.10 | 1 | | | | | | | | | No fires. Incendiaries extinguished | | | |
| 13-10-40 | 19.45 | 21.27 | Stoneferry and Kathleen Roads. Maxwell and Woodhall Streets | 20.20 | | 4 | | | | | | | 4 | Domestic and Industrial. Slight damage | I.D. | 2 | 8 |
| 22-10-40 | 01.44 | 02.58 | Sutton and Silverdale Roads. Maybury Road, Belfield Avenue | 01.40 | | | | | | | 2 | | 40 | Mine dropped before warning. Extensive damage | D. | | |
| 1-11-40 | 06.15 | 07.46 | Frodsham Street. Marfleet Avenue to Railway | 06.54 | | 12 | | | | | | | 12 | Domestic damage slight, hit on railway | R.D. | 1 | 7 |
| 7-11-40 | 18.56 | 20.42 | Incendiary raid only. Flinton Grove, Preston Road, Marfleet Lane | 19.00 | 1 | | | | | | | | | No fires started. Incendiaries extinguished | | | |
| 8-11-40 | 17.48 | 20.40 | Fairfax and Cranbrook Avenues, Cottingham Road, Newland Avenue | 18.00 | | 13 | | | | | | | 13 | Mainly in fields. Domestic damage | D. | | 2 |

| Date | Red Hrs. | White Hrs. | Area affected | Time of first bomb | Incendiaries (Clusters) | Ks. 50 cwt. 1 | Ks. 250 cwt. 5 | Ks. 500 cwt. 10 | Ks. 1000 cwt. 20 | Ks. 1800 cwt. 36 | Mines P.M. Ks. 1000 cwt. 20 | Mines G.M. Ks. 1000 cwt. 20 | Weight per raid in cwt. | Remarks | Damage | Casualties K. | Casualties S.I. |
|---|---|---|---|---|---|---|---|---|---|---|---|---|---|---|---|---|---|
| 11-11-40 | 17.39 | 18.09 | Maybury Road to City Boundary. | 17.52 | | 5 | | | | | | | 5 | Slight damage to domestic property | D. | | |
| 12-12-40 | 04.43 | 06.33 | Incendiary raid only. Hedon Road, Paragon Street and Bankside | 04.45 | 6 | | | | | | | | | Further warning. All incendiaries put out | | | |
| 17-12-40 | No warning | No warning | Incendiary raid only. Greek Street and Woodlands Road | 02.55 | 1 | | | | | | | | | No fires started | | | |
| 4/5-2-41 | 18.50 | 02.27 | Goddard Avenue | 23.10 | | | 2 | | | | | | 10 | Slight domestic damage | D. | 4 | |
| 11/12-2-41 | 17.28 | 17.50 | Jalland Street | 17.32 | | | | | | | | | | Anti-aircraft shell | | | |
| 14/15-2-41 | 19.00 | 02.10 | Glasshouse Row, Central Street | 19.00 | | 7 | | | | | | | 7 | Damage to oil mills and warehouses | I. | | 3 |
| 16-2-41 | 01.36 | 06.58 | Hedon Road, Tower House | 01.36 | | | 4 | | | | | | 20 | Fell in fields. No damage | | | |
| 22/23-2-41 | 19.30 | 22.38 | Rowlston and Ellerby Groves and Hawthorn Avenue | 19.30 | | | 1 | | | 1 | 2 | | 81 | 36 cwt. UXB rnear railway crossing not recovered. Extensive damage Rowlston Grove | R.D. | 4 | 4 |
| 23/24-2-41 | 19.14 | 01.03 | De la Pole Avenue, Hedon Road, Clough Road, Alexandra Dock | 19.14 | | | 4 | 2 | | | 3 | | 100 | Terrace damaged De le Pole Avenue. Mines exploded by sweeping | D. | 12 | 26 |
| 25-2-41 | 19.49 | 00.01 | Kirby Street. Incendiaries, North Hull | 20.00 | 4 | | 2 | | | | | | 10 | Incendiaries put out. One UXB removed 4-3-41 | | | 5 |
| 26-2-41 | No warning | No warning | Alexandra Dock, 12.02 hrs. | | | | | | | | 1 | | 20 | Mine dropped 23/24-2-41 sank lighters *Monarch* and *Brokelu* | I. | 1 | 1 |
| 1/2-3-41 | 19.45 | 23.50 | James Reckitt Avenue, East Park | 20.50 | | | | | | | 2 | | 40 | Domestic damage James Reckitt Avenue | D. | 5 | 5 |
| 13/14-3-41 | 20.56 | 04.26 | 5th Avenue Council School, North Hull and Stoneferry (Bridge Approach) | 20.36 | | 170 | 2 | | | | 2 | | 220 | Large fire at Sissons paint works | I.D. | 38 | 79 |
| 14/15-3-41 | 20.15 | 03.10 | Bean Street, St. Andrew's Dock, Stoneferry | 20.15 | | 1 | 1 | | | | 2 | | 46 | Mine at Bean Street. Extensive domestic damage | D. | 16 | 22 |
| 18/19-3-41 | 20.11 | 04.48 | Heavy raid. North Hull and Central Hull | 20.11 | | 134 | 111 | 17 | | | 5 | | 995 | Large fire at Sissons varnish works. Many bombs fell in fields | I.D. | 91 | 70 |
| 31/1-4-41 | 20.22 | 00.51 | Ferensway, Freehold Street, Boulevard, Hedon Road, Prospect Street, Priory Sidings | | | 2 | | | | | 12 | | 242 | Two UXM. Infirmary damaged. A.R.P. Control badly damaged | I.D.R. | 52 | 72 |
| 3/4-4-41 | 20.52 | 01.00 | East Hull area. Incendiary raid. | 22.00 | | | | | | | | | | All incendiaries put out | D. | 1 | |
| 7/8-4-41 | 21.02 | 04.97 | Spring Bank West, Kirklands Road | 00.38 | | | 1 | 1 | 1 | | | | 30 | 10 cwt. UXB exploded 8-4-41 at 16.00 hrs. | D. | | 1 |
| 9/10-4-41 | 23.07 | 05.06 | South-East and Central. Incendiary raid | 03.55 | 4 | | | | | | | | | All incendiaries put out | | | |

| Date | Red Hrs. | White Hrs. | Area affected | Time of first bomb | Incendiaries (Clusters) | Ks. 50 cwt. 1 | Ks. 250 cwt. 5 | Ks. 500 cwt. 10 | Ks. 1000 cwt. 20 | Ks. 1800 cwt. 36 | Mines P.M. Ks. 1000 cwt. 20 | Mines G.M. Ks. 1000 cwt. 20 | Weight per raid in cwt. | Remarks | Damage | Casualties K. | Casualties S.I. |
|---|---|---|---|---|---|---|---|---|---|---|---|---|---|---|---|---|---|
| 15/16-4-41 | 21.28 | 04.59 | Holdemess Road, Hedon Road and Alexandra Dock. Jennings Street | 03.30 | 3 | | | | | | 6 | | 120 | Ellis Terrace Shelter (50) disappeared. One fire at Jennings Street | I.D.R. | 57 | 20 |
| 23/24-4-41 | 21.29 | 23.34 | St. George's Road, Glasgow Street. | 22.40 | | | | | | | | | | Two A.A. shells came down and demolished two houses | D. | | |
| 25/26-4-11 | 21.25 | 23.49 | Council Avenue, Rokeby Avenue. | 22.50 | 2 | | | | | | 2 | | 40 | Mine fell on Housing Estate, West Hull | D. | 8 | 4 |
| 26/27-4-41 | 21.55 | 02.55 | Kingston High School and Lynton Avenue | 01.00 | | | | | | | 2 | | 40 | Mines in fields. Slight domestic damage | D. | | |
| 3/4-5-41 | 23.10 | 04.00 | Alexandra Dock, Marfleet Lane | 23.50 | | | | | | | 1 | 1 | 40 | First G. Mines dropped on Fenners, caught fire | I.R. | | 1 |
| 5/6-5-41 | 23.04 | 05.03 | King George Dock | 23.40 | | | 1 | | | | | | 5 | Damage to warehouse | R. | | |
| 7/8-5-41 | 23.16 | 05.08 | Riverside Quay, Shopping Centre, High Street. (Heavy raid) | 00.35 | 10 | 45 | 47 | 6 | | | 26 | 2 | 900 | Major fires, Riverside Quay, Shopping Centre | D.I.R. | 203 | 165 |
| 9-5-41 | 00.05 | 05.55 | King George, Alexandra and Victoria Docks, and East and North Hull. (Heavy raid.) | 00.10 | 12 | 113 | 49 | 24 | 4 | | 41 | 1 | 1518 | Major fires, Hedon Road and timber on docks | D.I.R. | 217 | 160 |
| 9/10-5-41 | 23.40 | 05.55 | Sutton | 01.20 | | | 3 | 1 | | | | | 25 | All fell in fields, no damage | | | |
| 12-5-41 | 00.20 | 03.45 | Clifton and Albany Streets. Beverley Road and Sutton | 01.15 | | 1 | 6 | | | | | | 31 | One UXB, bomb casing split open | D. | 2 | 3 |
| 28/29-5-41 | 00.12 | 04.50 | St. Andrew's Dock and Priory Sidings | 01.57 | 1 | | 2 | UXB 1 | | | | | 20 | No fires started, little damage | R. | | |
| 2-6-41 | 22.30 | 23.55 | Marlborough Avenue, Park Avenue, Blenheim Street, Margaret Street | 00.01 | | 2 | 2 | | | | | | 12 | Bombs dropped after "All Clear" | D. | 27 | 11 |
| 23-6-41 | 00.18 | 02.52 | Goddard Avenue | 01.26 | | 6 | | | | | | | 6 | Slight domestic damage | D. | | |
| 29-6-41 | 01.27 | 03.33 | East Hull and King George Dock. Slight damage | 01.45 | 5 | 50 | | | | | | | 50 | Stoneferry Bridge hit. All fires put out | D. | 1 | 5 |
| 9/10-6-41 | 00.12 | 02.53 | Incendiary raid only. East Hull | 00.38 | | | | | | | | | | All incendiaries put out | I.D.R. | | |
| 11-7-41 | 00.53 | 03.05 | General attack. North of railway approach to station | 01.15 | 6 | 28 | 18 | 6 | 3 | | | 1 | 258 | One major fire, Blundell Spence. Aire Street. All other fires put out | I.D.R. | 21 | 46 |
| 15-7-41 | 00.55 | 03.19 | North Hull Estate, Anlaby Road, Sidmouth Street | 01.50 | | 9 | 8 | 5 | 3 | | | 5 | 259 | School damaged. Only domestic property | D. | 25 | 28 |
| 18-7-41 | 01.18 | 04.07 | Heavy raid. East Hull and Victoria Dock | 01.20 | 4 | 92 | 55 | 21 | 4 | | | 3 | 717 | Large fires at Spillers and East Hull Gas, Reckitts | I.D. | 140 | 108 |
| 23-7-41 | 00.09 | 03.25 | Holdemess Road, Holland Street, Preston Road | 00.35 | | 3 | 3 | 2 | | | | | 35 | Mainly shop and domestic property | D. | 2 | 5 |

| Date | Red Hrs. | White Hrs. | Area affected | Time of first bomb | Incendiaries (Clusters) | Ks. 50 cwt. 1 | Ks. 250 cwt. 5 | Ks. 500 cwt. 10 | Ks. 1000 cwt. 20 | Ks. 1800 cwt. 36 | Mines P.M. Ks. 1000 cwt. 20 | Mines G.M. Ks. 1000 cwt. 20 | Weight per raid in cwt. | Remarks | Damage | Casualties K. | Casualties S.I. |
|---|---|---|---|---|---|---|---|---|---|---|---|---|---|---|---|---|---|
| 18-8-41 | 02.10 | 03.50 | Central and mainly East Hull. Domestic | 02.05 | | 5 | 9 | 4 | 2 | | | | 130 | Three shelters damaged | I.D. | 20 | 15 |
| 3-9-41 | 22.07 | 02.32 | S.W., Central and mainly East Hull | 22.30 | | 1 | 4 | 8 | 2 | | | | 141 | Mainly domestic, 16 shelters damaged | I.D. | 44 | 36 |
| 21-9-41 | 01.21 | 03.52 | Priory Sidings, Hessle Road | 01.35 | 1 | 5 | | | | | | | 5 | Slight damage to four tracks | R. | | |
| 12/13-10-41 | 23.02 | 02.58 | Across Humber Dock (fragments found) | 00.11 | | | | 4 | | | | | 40 | Two further warnings, Red 20.43, White 22.53, and Red 03.30, White 03.59 | R. | | 2 |
| 7/8-11-41 | 21.23 | 00.09 | Airlie Street, St. Matthew Street, Coltman Street and Bean Street | 22.58 | | | | 4 | | | | | 40 | Strong ground stock | D. | | |
| 13/14-1-42 | 23.31 | 01.32 | Willerby Road, Woodlands Road, Springhead Avenue | 00.05 | | | 1 | 2 | | | | | 25 | One Bay, Willerby Road, turned over | D. | 4 | 5 |
| 1-5-42 | 03.20 | 04.40 | Bank Street, Victoria Street, Railway south of Botanic Crossing | 03.30 | | | | 3 | | | | | 30 | Deep penetration. Railway damaged | R.D. | 7 | 5 |
| 19/20-5-42 | 23.39 | 01.16 | Scarborough Street, Westbourne Avenue, Sutton, Southcoates Lane, Alexandra Dock | 00.04 | 4 | 4 | 14 | 54 | 1 | 1 | | | 670 | Fires on dock and Southcoates Lane, extensive damage Scarborough Street | I.R.D. | 10 | 12 |
| 31/1-8-42 | 02.15 | 03.25 | Grindell Street and Victoria Dock | 02.42 | | | | 1 | | 1 | | | 46 | Extensive domestic damage | R.D. | | |
| 24/25-10-42 | 21.10 | 22.48 | Campbell Street, Walker Street, Anlaby Road near Paragon Station | 21.40 | | | | 4 | | | | | 40 | Damage not serious | R.D. | 3 | 7 |
| 20/21-12-42 | 19.31 | 20.15 | Tunis Street, Holderness Road, Staveley Road, Carden Avenue, Bilton Grove | 19.25 | | | | 7 | | | | | 70 | Damage to domestic property | D. | 3 | 10 |
| 3/4-1-43 | 20.35 | 21.32 | Bankside of River Hull and Sissons Wharf | 20.30 | | | | 2 | | | | | 20 | Length of timber wharf demolished | I. | | |
| 15/16-1-43 | 20.08 | 21.33 | Marfleet Lane, Bilton Grove to Stanhope Avenue | 21.00 | 9 | | | 2 | | | | | 20 | Damage to domestic property | D. | | |
| 23/24-6-43 | 02.35 | 03.31 | Widespread areas. Brunswick Avenue, Holderness Road, Mytongate | 02.37 | 8 | 2 | | 11 | 4 | | | | 192 | Damage fairly widespread | D.I.R. | | |
| 13/14-7-43 | 01.22 | 02.13 | Areas widespread, sharp attack | 01.23 | 3 | 35 | | 41 | 6 | | | | 565 | Damage widespread | D.I.R. | 26 | 28 |
| 4-3-45 | | | Areas widespread | | | | No. Phosphorous bombs | | | | | | | | Damage not serious | D.I. | | |
| 17/18-3-45 | 21.36 | 22.30 | Holderness Road, Morrill Street, Holland Street | | | Numerous cannon shells | | 37 No. S.D.10 37 No. S.D.19 | | | | | | 21½ | Little damage | D. | 12 | 22 |

NOTE.—The above Schedule includes occurrences only within the City boundaries. There were several raids in which incidents occurred in the immediate vicinity of the City, some of which are referred to elsewhere in the Book. Plane crashes in the City are not included.